"Every once in a while a book comes around to snap us out of our mediocrity and put us back on the path of our purpose and calling. *An Unashamed Life* is just that! These stories remind us that our lives matter and God is always working—in the tragedies and triumphs and even the mundane details of everyday life. God is definitely not finished with us yet!"

Victorya Rogers

Life Coach, Co-Author "How to Talk About Jesus without Freaking Out"

An Unashamed Life

24 Stories Proclaiming the Transformational Power of Jesus Christ

"Uphold me according to Your word, that I may live;
And do not let me be ashamed of my hope."

– Psalm 119:116

Jerry A Chavez

Thrilling Life Publishers
Southlake, Texas

An Unashamed Life
Published by Thrilling Life Publishers
P.O. Box 92522
Southlake, TX 76092
www.thrillinglife.com

Printed in the United States of America
International Standard Book Number: 978-0-9849220-5-5

Cover design by Jerry A Chavez
Cover images by Crowd Silhouette Image and Shutterstock.com
Edited by Felicia Chavez

Scripture quotations are from:
The Holy Bible, New King James Version © 1979, 1980, 1982
by Thomas Nelson, Inc., Used by Permission

Thrilling Life Publishers
Inspiration
Helping you Pursue a Thrilling Life – John 10:10
www.thrillinglife.com
www.thrillinglife.com/unashamedlife

"The key is the Gospel changes lives and the speaker's stories reflect His workings"

Terence Chatmon

President and CEO | Fellowship of Companies for Christ International, FCCI

"We are all called to be disciples and telling our stories is part of what God wants us to do! We need to keep telling our stories so that we can glorify the Lord and tell others how God turns all things into good for those who love Him!"

Karen Covell

Founding Director | Hollywood Prayer Network

"This ministry is VERY important for we see and hear stories of how God is working in our midst today. I work in prisons and often the unchurched think the Bible is filled with stories of people who lived thousands of years ago. Hearing these speakers share their stories in *An Unashamed Life* and at the Testify World Conferences proves that He is just as alive and active today as He was with the disciples 2,000 years ago."

Ann Edenfield

Executive Director and Founder | Wings for LIFE International

"The younger generation needs to hear such stories as these and by hearing be stimulated to go for it themselves and share their testimonies, in turn accomplishing the unique mission the Lord has for each one."

John Robb

Chairman | International Prayer Council

"The world craves evidence that it is worthy of being loved, especially by a God whom it fears exists only to judge its failures—if He exists at all. It cries out for relief from a painful existence while dying daily for lack of hope that life can be different. What I experienced in Testify World validates a truth I once read: The greatest conductor of spiritual energy is human flesh. Each of these true stories in *An Unashamed Life* flesh out undeniable evidence of God's love and power to change. As a participant, I am convinced that Testify World needs to spread this hope—city by city—across our nation to meet our world's need. For it is through flesh and blood testimonies like these that an invisible kingdom not only becomes visible, but expands."

Kitty Chappell

Award Winning Author & International Speaker

This book is dedicated to my two amazing daughters,
Mariah and Christina,
who fill my every breath and fuel my every motivation.

TABLE OF CONTENTS

FORWARD

As a producer in Hollywood I live my life helping people to tell stories. So when Jerry A Chavez approached me and said he was compiling a book of personal stories about encounters with God I got excited. Stories are the most powerful tool man can use to touch the heart of another person. Jesus is our role model as the best storyteller ever known. The best pastors I know tell stories. Salesmen, filmmakers and parents all tell stories. People spend hours a day watching stories on television and they listen to stories through music. Book lovers devour one story after the next, slipping into the worlds that they are reading about. My children would want to hear a good story over and over again, never getting tired of it and always wanting more. And when I share my faith, I tell stories. Ingmar Bergman, the great Swedish screenwriter and film director once said, "Facts go straight to the head, but stories go straight to the heart." I'm so convinced of that that I co-authored a book, "How to Talk About Jesus Without Freaking Out," about how Christians can share our faith with others by telling stories.

Christians should be ready to give an account for the truth that they have within them, with gentleness and reverence. This book is full of people's stories. And the beauty of these stories is that there is no excuse that can be used to say that they were mistranslated through the generations or they were misinterpreted. They are empirical truth, dramatic and powerful, told by the people who experienced them and they are all about our mysterious, life-changing, unconditionally loving God who created the universe. So read them, and pass them on to someone you know who might just need to read a good story about God that will go straight to their heart!"

Karen Covell

Producer, Author and Founding Director of

The Hollywood Prayer Network

ACKNOWLEDGEMENTS

My amazingly talented sister Felicia Chavez for her skillful editing

Thrilling Life Publishers--
partnering with you is a blessing

The Testify World family of speakers, supporters and volunteers--
our partnership with you is deeply appreciated

INTRODUCTION

Jerry A Chavez

"But none of these things move me; nor do I count my life dear to myself, so that I may finish my race with joy, and the ministry which I received from the Lord Jesus, to Testify to the Gospel of the Grace of God."
– Acts 20:24

As a follower of Jesus Christ I have come to realize the amazing power of testimony. That's why we've developed Testify World, a global community of kingdom builders who share the transformational power of Jesus Christ. This not-for-profit ministry is dedicated to "Making the Invisible Kingdom VISIBLE."

Testify World is where the art of storytelling meets the power of testimony. Every year, the world's servant leaders gather to share the amazing work the Lord accomplishes in their lives and the lives of others. Told live and without notes, each story is true, each voice authentic.

There are countless stories around the world that need telling. We aim to inspire a new generation of evangelistic outreach by which it is possible to have hundreds of communities share stories that can spawn into films, TV shows, and new media. By giving people a venue to share their story on a global platform, we are inspiring communities from around the world.

This book is a compilation of stories from those who have encountered the reality of Jesus Christ. They were presented at various Testify World outreach events around the country and have been transcribed, edited, and formatted for publication.

Our prayer is that these testimonies will serve as a resource for fellow pilgrims passing through this world as both a witness unto others and a source of encouragement for seasons of testing.

MIGHTY MAN OF GOD

Michael K. Reynolds

And the Angel of the Lord appeared to him,
and said to him,
"The Lord is with you, you mighty man of valor!"
– Judges 6:12

When I was younger, I wanted to be great. I wanted to be a rock star. Because, let's face it, ever since we were kids we craved significance. Maybe we wanted to be an astronaut or a football star. None of us ever cradled a doll and said, "I want to be a mediocre mom."

I pursued greatness with vehemence. At 15-years-old, I decided that I was going to be a best-selling author. Two years later, I'd written my first novel. It was so good that when a friend offered to read it, I never asked for it back. Hopefully it's in a landfill now. My second novel - now *that* was where I was going to solve all of the puzzles of the universe. The only problem was, I never finished it. By 20, I was on my fourth novel, "Flight of the Earls." So when I applied to a graduate writing program and wasn't accepted, I was really discouraged. It was the first time in my life when things weren't going my way. I felt like all the doors were closed. That's when God intervened in my life.

My walk with God was so new and exciting. But I wanted to be a rock star again, a Mighty Man of God. That way I could still be great, but in the name of God. I started my own business, a godly business. We donated 50% of our work to churches so that I would be honored as a Mighty Man of God. But I was a fake. I was well-respected in the community as a great servant, yet my staff hated me. I had a failing business partnership. My wife resented the business because I was borrowing to give. I was at a breaking point.

God took me to a peacemaker's organization with my business partner. I arrived with a stack of papers, evidence to explain all of the great things I had done and why I was right in our dispute. Fifteen minutes into the process, God brought me to my knees. I spent the next two hours apologizing to my business partner for the many ways I had wronged him. Just when I thought I was finished, God gave me a scroll of other things for which I needed to apologize. In that moment, I learned four words: I might be wrong. Other people are as important as I am? It was amazing.

It was at this point that I got involved in a community project. Some 80% of crime in our neighborhood resulted from meth addiction. My business volunteered to make posters for area schools. Posters grew into commercials. One day, a general manager of the local TV station asked, "Have you ever thought of doing a 30-minute documentary and airing it at a roadblock?" A roadblock is when all of the stations block out airtime, just like during the President's State of the Union address. He continued, "Of course, none of the general managers will agree to it."

I thought, "This is more work than I was going to volunteer, but it sounds like a good idea." I went to the first general manager prepared with my pitch. Within five minutes, he stopped me and said, "We're on board." I went to the next general manager. Within five minutes, he stopped me and said, "We're on board." All of the general managers agreed to air an anti-meth documentary on all of the TV stations. The only problem was, we didn't have a documentary.

In three months, I saw God's amazing work. I intended to film a long list of people who were out of jail, but they didn't show up. We were down to one young lady named Tenille who had lived a life beyond hell. As she shared her story, it was a pivotal moment. God was ready to do something great with someone broken. From Tenille's interview, we ended up making the documentary. The first time that the TV stations ever saw it was the day before it aired. God intervened and people came together like nothing we've ever seen. It was the most watched program of all time in our community.

Afterward, I was relieved. I was done! But God wasn't finished. The First Lady of Nevada said, "Hey, you did this for Northern Nevada. You're going to get me in trouble if you don't do it for Southern Nevada." We did the campaign in Las Vegas and then Oregon, Sacramento, and San Diego. In Arizona, 62 TV stations aired the documentary. We went on to New Mexico, El Paso, and Ciudad Juarez. God protected us as we filmed "In the Ghettos of Ciudad Juarez." Ultimately, the Mexican government edited the documentary themselves, so it wasn't my program at all. And do you know what? It didn't matter because God was in charge. From there it was Sonora, Mexico, Colorado, and Oklahoma, where over half the population watched the documentary.

Throughout this process, I witnessed incredible darkness. A mother selling her eight-year-old child to prostitution to pay drug debts. Children doing drugs with their mom in an effort to connect. Suicide. I learned how small my troubles were, and in what great a capacity God used me. We had people come to us from New Zealand, Russia, and South Korea, all because God had used someone who was broken, someone who knew that greatness wasn't the goal.

Years later, a friend invited me to a writer's conference. I hadn't written a single word of fiction in 20 years. Sitting across the table from an editor, for whatever reason God gave me the courage to pitch my old novel, "Flight of the Earls." As an introduction, I said, "I'm a producer of a documentary that has impacted more than 30 million people and won an Emmy." The agent said, "I'm listening." I pitched the novel and praise God, I have a writing contract for a trilogy. What I'm most excited about is that my work is going to be of God. Even though Mighty Man of God *sounds* good - the Mighty Man part, the Mighty Woman part, the great mom, the great writer - it's all of God. I have to ask myself daily, hourly, and by the minute, "We are all willing to lay our burdens at the foot of the cross. Are we willing to lay our desires?" Amen.

Michael K. Reynolds

Michael K. Reynolds is a writer with more than two decades of experience in crafting fiction, non-fiction, journalism, copywriting and documentary production. He is also the producer of the Emmy and Telly Award Winning documentary called Crystal Darkness which so far has been viewed by more than 10 million people with its accompanying campaigns reaching in excess of 30 million to date.

Learn More: www.michaelkreynolds.com

TRANSFORMING HEARTS AND HEADLINES

John Robb

"If My people who are called by My name will humble themselves, and pray and seek My face, and turn from their wicked ways, then I will hear from heaven, and will forgive their sin and heal their land."
– 2 Chronicles 7:14

A number of years ago, a visiting speaker presented at World Vision, a Christian humanitarian organization. He arrested us with his question: "Are you doing a program for the Lord or welcoming the presence of the Lord?" That stopped me in my tracks. I was so busy carrying out my own agenda, often depending on my own strength and effort. Scripture warns us about that, doesn't it?

I was burned out. At the suggestion of my boss, I went away for a two-day retreat at a Benedictine monastery in the California desert. In all that silence, God's voice became a megaphone in my heart: "Don't think you're impressing me with all the things you're doing for me." I'd been all over the world, doing all kinds of ministry for Him, and here He was saying, "It really doesn't impress me that much. What I'm really after is intimacy with you. You're my child. That's what I value." And then He said, "Get out of my way. Let me be your senior partner and you will see my wonders."

Henri Nouwen, in his profound little book called "The Way of the Heart," said, "Solitude is the furnace of transformation." Those two days of encounter alone with the Lord shifted my whole ministry. I started to get invitations to take prayer leaders into warzones, places that were indescribably chaotic. We gathered as Christian leaders across the spectrum. We threw away our agendas and simply sought to be present to the Lord. In return, we asked Him to be present to us. We prayed for the healing and transformation of those nations. And we saw such amazing wonders happen, we couldn't believe it.

Cambodia was one of the first. The Khmer Rouge had killed two million of their own people to enact their "utopian" vision. In 1995, we took a team to facilitate three days of prayer with Cambodian Christian Leaders. We asked intercessory networks to pray that the Khmer Rouge would dissolve. Three months later, The New York Times reported that The Khmer Rouge were dissolving. Where there had once been division, a united National Christian fellowship came into being for the first time. Across the country, people began to come to the Lord; the church grew from 10,000 to an estimated 400,000 in just a few years.

Later that year, I was invited to take a team into Bosnia, where three ethnic groups were at war. 250,000 people had died in the conflict. Hundreds of thousands of people had been made homeless. Together with the locals, meeting behind a wall of sandbags piled high over the windows for protection from sniper fire, our team facilitated a time of deep reconciliation prayer for the nation's healing. One woman stood up with tears streaming down her face. "Forgive us Serbs for what we have done to you Croats," she said. And the Croats were so impacted that they stood up, three of them, and said, "No, we're worse than you Serbs." Then, all, including those believers from the Muslim ethnic background, threw their arms around one another, weeping and confessing the corporate sins and atrocities that had torn the nation apart. Together we held hands and agreed in the name of Jesus that peace would come to Bosnia. Within four days, Milosevic, the hardened dictator, put forth a peace proposal. The U.S. diplomat said, "I don't know what softened him." That peace proposal resulted in the Dayton Peace Accords that ended the war a few months later. Thanks be to the Lord!

Afghanistan. We took a team into the country in 1999 while the Taliban were in power. We gathered in a stadium where sports were no longer played; it was now used to cut off the limbs of petty criminals, to shoot women who spoke with men to whom they were not related. We confessed the blood guilt before the Lord. We prayed. Thousands prayed around the world. To the glory of the Lord, there was never another amputation or execution in that stadium! Everything else we prayed for was also later granted. The Taliban were overthrown, women's rights were restored, children were able to go back to school. Now, after considerable progress by the nation and its government, we need to keep praying for Afghanistan because the Taliban are waging a fierce guerilla war to reclaim power.

In 2010, we were involved with a prayer initiative in Mexico. President Calderon, a secular president, was convinced that Mexico would lose the war against the drug cartels except through prayer. He invited evangelical pastors and international prayer leaders to pray for his nation. The next day, headlines read that they had arrested a drug lord known as the "king of heroin". A whole nationwide prayer movement has developed in Mexico and God has been answering. The Mexican government has arrested or otherwise eliminated the majority of the 37 most wanted drug kingpins since God's people there and around the world began to pray specifically about those on that list. Praise the Lord for His faithfulness.

God can and will heal hearts and nations. We've all heard that famous verse in 2 Chronicles 7:14. In 60 national prayer initiatives, my colleagues and I have witnessed this promise fulfilled over and over again, even in many horrendous and hopeless situations of human conflict and suffering. It's not just serendipity. If we come to Him, if we unite our prayer, He will answer. Prayer connects us to the awesome greatness of God. Rather than knocking ourselves out trying to make things the way we want them to be, shouldn't we submit to Him? Shouldn't we say, "We're going to ask you, Lord God, the one who has all power, to fix these situations because they are beyond our solution, hopeless and impossible."

So, how can we grow in transformational prayer? First, find a prayer partner. One of my prayer partners is my wife of 44 years. Another is a dear friend of 27 years. The three of us could fill an encyclopedia with all of the answers we've received in prayer. Second, make it a practice to dwell in the presence of God as you go through your day. Talk with Him about everything. Prayer should be as natural as breathing. Not a religious duty, but a delight. Enjoy Him. Listen. Prayer is not a monologue. Finally, be childlike. Pray simply and from the heart. We don't have to give God a lecture. He wants us to come to Him in a simple, heartfelt way.

A Christian astrophysicist once said, "Because prayer is extra dimensional in its reach, it must be considered the most powerful capacity God has made available to us." And it's true. We exercise our God-given authority through prayer. We've been raised up, scripture says, to sit with Jesus Christ in the heavenly places. We're already there. We're sitting beside Him whether we know it or not. Let's therefore use the authority He grants us to affect real change on our planet through united, faith-filled prayer. Pray about the issues in your community and across the world. As we do, God can and will change both hearts and headlines!

Amen.

John Robb

John Robb serves as Chairman for the International Prayer Council, and International Prayer Connect, a network of regional and national prayer ministries and networks around the world. The IPC focuses on global issues of common concern to the Body of Christ such as war, terrorism, and other humanitarian issues as well as on the fulfillment of Christ's Great Commandment and the completion of the Great Commission.

Learn More: www.ipcprayer.org

THROWAWAYS

Tim Gamwell

"And the King will answer and say to them,
'Assuredly, I say to you, inasmuch
as you did it to one of the least of these My brethren,
you did it to Me.'
– Matthew 25:40

When I was five-years-old, my family lived in a little village in the mountains of Chihuahua, Mexico. Every night when the sun went down, all of the doors and windows locked. I'd peak through the crack in the door and see men drinking cervezas, yelling and shooting their guns in the air. The town was full of murderers. It was the outlaws' hideaway. We lived there because my parents were missionaries. They'd moved to Mexico in the late 1940's by faith. They believed Jesus when he said, "As you've done to the least of these, you've done it to me."

As missionaries, we travelled from one village to the next, always staying wherever we could. Sometimes it was out in the field, sometimes it was in an empty house. Wherever we were, you'd best guarantee there were people in need. My mom and dad were always ministering to others.

Sometimes it seemed like my mom was cooking for the whole village, yet she still found time to visit every home, pray for every family. As I grew up I learned that we're all missionaries. We're all in it together. I had seven brothers and sisters and we all shared in the mission work. Our purpose in life was to honor God and share His love.

When I got older, I didn't have any intention of going back to Mexico. My wife and I worked with youth, the street kids of El Paso. We ministered to runaways, homeless, prostitutes, and drug addicts. But God led me to take some of our youth back to Mexico to visit an orphanage. We saw the great need and felt like we had to do something. I began to work more predominantly in Mexico than in the United States.

One day, as I was returning home from an orphanage, I met a 9-year-old girl named Graciella. She was begging. I asked her where she was from and she said Guatemala. I said, "You come up here with mommy and daddy?" And she said, "No, I came up here in the big truck with all the little girls." She had a friend with her who was doubled up in pain. I said, "Your friend needs help. Do you want me to take her to a doctor?" Graciella said, "You can't help her. She's going to die. She has AIDS."

It hit me. These girls were beggars during the day and child prostitutes at night. For every child we helped in the orphanage, there were a thousand more on the street. I wondered if we could take our program to the street to reach the children before they became statistics. I built community centers that provided for the whole family: vocational training and after-school programs and medical clinics, whatever the people needed. The Lord continued to guide us. Youth groups and mission groups helped us administer and build.

One day, I took one of these youth groups with me to the plaza to minister Christ's love. I also took kids from one of the shelters that housed child prostitutes. I wanted them to learn the story of how God saved them, and at the same time, to learn to serve God, to share God's passion. I asked a 14-year-old to share her story. She took the mic. "When I was 10-years old," she said, "I was a prostitute and a drug addict. I used to sleep under that bench. I had no life, no purpose, no direction. Nobody cared about me. But today, God has changed all that. I have a life, I have purpose, and I have direction. He can do the same for you if you give Him a chance." Everybody in the plaza stopped to listen as she preached.

After our program, a man said, "Would you mind if I address your group for a moment?" I said, "Okay." I didn't know who he was, but I love a good adventure. "50 years ago," he said, "my mommy answered the door and there was a man who wanted to talk about God. She invited him into our home. In the end, she accepted Christ as her savior. The man gave her a Bible and said, 'Study the word to know God. Open your heart and your home to serve him.' Today, my whole family serves the Lord. We work in orphanages and rehabs and churches in every major city in Chihuahua. My children, my nieces, my nephews, my brothers and sisters are all missionaries and pastors and evangelists. I thank the Lord every day for that man who knocked on our door, but I never had a chance to thank that man personally. So, thank you. That man was Tim's father." Well, how cool was that? To see the fruit of one little seed planted 50 years ago?

In my heart, I still thought about Graciella, that little 9-year-old girl I had met on the street. I began searching for runaways. I found throwaways instead. One of the girls, Leticia, had no father. Her mother was a drug addict and the men that she brought home would abuse her as well. Finally, she ran away with nowhere to go. So God led us to open a home. That home had just 10 girls when we opened it; today, there's over 90 boys and girls. Leticia is now serving the Lord in Canada with her husband and their two beautiful children.

We've seen the power of God's work, a power even violence couldn't stop. When it got so bad that the shops closed and people hid in their homes, when the missionaries stopped coming and everyone was fearful, God led us to preach the gospel and do concerts on the street. We've done about 150 concerts every year for the past six years. That's a lot of crusades.

The Lord has now provided the opportunity for us to open another home, a home for girls rescued from very bad situations. I'm going to share a little bit about one child so that you may understand. At 13-years-old, one girl was abducted and raped by a gang. They slit her throat and left her for dead. By God's providence she survived. She spent more than a year in the hospital. She used to wear a bandana around her neck to hide the scar, but today she wears no bandana. She praises the Lord for her life and goes to school.

One day, one of our girls said, "Why do the mission groups come over to Mexico and help the Mexicans?" I said, "Well honey, Jesus said, 'As you've done to the least of these, you've done to me.' In other words, if you don't care about those that I love, don't tell me that you love me." I went on to share a story with her from my childhood.

In this one village growing up, there was a man named Pompeii. Everyone called him *loco,* crazy. He was always coming to our house. My mom would invite him in and give him a plate of food. He'd scarf it down and leave the house singing, a big smile on his face. But one day he scarfed the food down with no smile. My mom said, "Pompeii, where's your smile?" He lifted up his pant leg. His leg was swollen with infection.

My mom sat down at his feet. She cleaned out the maggots and pus, then medicated and bandaged his leg. And do you know what happened? Pompeii's smile came back. He left the house singing. But as soon as he walked out the door, my little sister said, "Mom that was so gross. How could you do that?" My mom answered like she always did. "Honey, how can we not do such little things for our Lord Jesus who did so much for us?"

My mom shared the heart of Christ. And we have the same opportunity to share his heart, too, to understand what he meant when he said, "Surely I say unto to you, as you have done unto the least of these my brethren, you have done unto me." Amen.

Tim Gamwell

Timothy Gamwell is a product of a family legacy of missions and currently serves as the director of Life Challenge International, a non-profit Christian charitable organization serving the Juarez/El Paso border area and future missionaries around the world.

.

Learn More: www.lifechallenge.net

MASK

Saundra Crockett

"And we know that all things work together
for good to those who love God,
to those who are the called according to His purpose."
– Romans 8:28

I was born in Korea, the youngest of probably 12 children. I say 'probably' because I don't know. I was told that there were 12 children and that most of them passed away before I was born. When I was four-years-old, my father who had loved me, who loved mountain climbing and who hiked with me, had a heart attack and passed away in my arms. That was the beginning of the change in my life. My mother thought it was better for me to be raised by my sister and her husband, an American. He was in the service and would give me a better life than I was living in Korea. We traveled all over the world. He helped me with my homework. He taught me how to play golf. He was a good man.

It wasn't until later that I realized he wasn't a great father, he was a great manipulator. He would manipulate me into thinking that he loved me. And because he loved me, it was okay for him to molest me. He molested me, but he always asked first if it was okay. I gave him permission to do what he did, and so I felt guilty. I carried that guilt for many years. When I finally told my sister, she denied it, which was worse than the molestation. For a long time I really hated them both. I wished I could run away.

I was 12-years-old when they divorced. My sister and I came to California to start life over. She went back to work after 10 years of being a housewife, leaving me alone to raise myself. During those years I escaped into books, mostly romance novels. My goal in life was to find the perfect husband, the man who would change my life for the better. I thought that was what real love was.

At 16-years-old, I met a boy I thought I loved. Together we lived a life in the streets, doing drugs to numb our pain. Now, living in the streets, there are some horrible things that could happen to you. The horrible things that could happen, did happen. I was raped, kidnapped - you think it, it happened. I don't know how I got through except that I didn't see any other options.

At 19-years-old, I had a daughter, which just intensified the pain because I didn't want to be a parent. I didn't know how to be a parent. I just wanted the pain to stop. The father was a very mean, angry person. I got to the point where I couldn't care less if he was hit by a bus; I would just walk over his body. By the time we broke up, it didn't mean anything to me.

I went on to marry another man who I thought was different. He wasn't. On my 28th birthday, I caught him with another woman. He was so upset that he assaulted me, left me in the street unconscious. He was a six-foot-two ex-marine, so you can imagine his punches were pretty significant. He hit me so hard that it started an internal infection. I lost the whole right side of my face to that infection. I was in the hospital for six months.

I had a child with this man, a son who was only two-years-old and so scared of my face that he wouldn't come near me. That really broke my heart. Dealing with the divorce and the loss of my face was incredibly difficult. I had, I don't know, 26 surgeries. I wore a surgical mask for 12 years. I ate with it on, I slept with it on. It was my way of hiding from the world. But that wasn't rock bottom. I hit rock bottom later, when I lost my children, my home, and what little was left of my reputation, to drugs.

When I lost custody of my children, I was also arrested. Two ladies from church, who had once led me in the sinner's prayer even though I didn't really know what it was, showed up in court and said that they would stand up for me. I didn't even know these people. It was the beginning of seeing Jesus in the flesh, understanding the love of Christ. It wasn't right away. I still made a lot of mistakes. I was in a Christian Women's shelter for six-and-a-half years. I had another little girl and I saw her as God sees us. God sees us as His children. And through my church, full of people with grace and love, God gave me a family. They helped me raise my children. They helped me believe in myself.

One day, while I was at a church retreat, this minister from Thailand prayed for me. The only thing she said was, "God loves you." I had heard that many, many times but for some reason the timing was right. When she said those words, I took off the surgical mask and never put it on again. I took that mask off and took a chance at going back to school, took a chance at going back to work. When I didn't believe in myself, the people from church believed in me. I never thought I could be anything in life, but now I am a teacher of His grace. I am God's redemption. I can laugh every day instead of cry because even though my life isn't perfect, it is full of love and grace due to the power of Jesus Christ. Amen.

Saundra Crockett

Saundra Crockett has been on her own since she was 16, living a life on the streets. Her story takes a big turn when her ex-husband assaulted her leaving her disfigured for life. Saundra's journey is a powerful example of forgiveness as she found the strength In Christ to move forward from this horrible circumstance. Saundra says, "Today I see things differently than most people do, only because of how God's love saved me."

THE CAVE

Anita Chavez

"Restore to me the joy of Your salvation,
And uphold me by Your generous Spirit."
– Psalm 51:12

My story starts in the year 2000, when I went to see my primary care doctor complaining of feeling blue. He put me on antidepressants. I went back again complaining that the pills weren't working, so he upped the dosage. I took even more pills. I went back to see him again, complaining that my heart was pounding so hard it felt like it was in my throat. He gave me more pills but I went back to crying, feeling blue. Eventually he referred me to a psychiatrist. She tried all kinds of stuff. Maybe some yoga, or how about pilates? A CD of Tibetan bells? Meditation? How about group therapy, talk therapy? But it wasn't working.

Six months later, I woke up tied to a hospital gurney in the mental health hospital. I asked a nurse, "What am I doing here?" She said, "Honey, you've tried to hurt yourself. We're here to help you." I closed my eyes and thought, "Suicide watch again. Not again." I needed to use the bathroom, but as I swung my legs from the gurney

I saw piles of brown and black cockroaches covering the floor. I screamed and yelled for the nurse. "The roaches, can't you see the roaches?" I asked. "There's nothing on the floor," she said.

She escorted me to the bathroom. I needed to splash water on my face, but when I turned on the faucet, out poured black spiders instead of water. I pounded my fists on the pretend mirror. I said, "God, I can't do this anymore. It's too much." I was screaming when the nurses and doctors came in. They gave me injections so that I could stay sane for just a few more minutes.

The doctors presented my family with a choice. "You can either keep her in the mental health hospital indefinitely or she can undergo ECT treatments – Electrical Convulsive Therapy." My family asked, "Will she be able to come home and be with us?" They said, "Yes. She'll start her treatments here and then she'll be able to go home."

I started shock therapy. They would take me to "the cave" – that's what the nurses and doctors nicknamed the ECT unit. It was dark, it was cold, and it was impersonable. They would wake me and the other patients up at 5 am. We would walk single file through the hospital and into the cave. We would lie on gurnies and wait for the doctors. Sometimes we would wait for two hours or more for treatment. We were low priority.

At the time, I was taking 13 different pills in conjunction with the ECTs. Pills upon pills upon pills to help with the physical side effects of ECT: horrific headaches and bodily pain, like I was beaten with a baseball bat. The procedure also erases your memory. The doctors would say, "No, it's not the ECT that's erasing your memory. It's the distress from your depression." But blocks of my memory are gone because of medication and ECTs.

I was diagnosed with major depression. Depression is really just another word for hopelessness. I was void of all emotion. I was diagnosed with schizophrenia, which meant that I was paranoid. Paranoid that my husband was trying to kill me, that my sister hated me. We would go to the grocery store and I would end up crouched in a corner because I thought that everyone was staring at me. And I was diagnosed with psychosis; I heard voices and saw visions like cockroaches, spiders, the man and woman who would appear at my kitchen window telling me what pills to take, what knives to use to cut my wrist. This is an excerpt from my journal at the time: *"I am in there somewhere – crying in my heart, please let me depart."* I just wanted relief, and if that meant hurting myself, then that's what it meant.

One day, we got a visit from a water softener saleslady. She did her presentation and then asked if I'd like to buy the product. I said, "No, I can't afford it," and she said, "Why not? We have payment plans available." I told her that I was on disability, that I had major depression and schizophrenia and psychosis. "Anita, you're too young to be on disability," she said. "You need to get off those pills."

I said, "There's more." I would count constantly, count to one hundred as I rocked, wringing my hands, running my fingers through my hair. I would count as I walked, as I brushed my teeth, as I did the dishes. It helped keep me sane. And I would cut my wrist until the blood renewed me. And I would eat and then vomit for relief from this horrible, horrible pit that I was stuck in.

"Get off the pills Anita," the saleslady repeated. "Get off the pills." She didn't even know me. It was like God telling me, "Have you given up on me? Have you lost hope? Are you believing these lies that they're telling you?" That night I flushed 12 of the 13 pills down the toilet. I said, "I'm not doing this anymore, not ECT and not the pills."

Three months later, I was back at work. It wasn't easy. It was very, very difficult to come back into the world after that kind of madness. It was spiritual warfare.

I'm not telling you this to be a horrific storyteller, but so that you understand the grace of

God, His mercy, His long suffering. His love for us is absolutely true. It's not just a book called "the Bible," it's the living word. He granted me a message for women who suffer from depression, to let you know that there is hope beyond what the world tells you, hope beyond what your family or friends or doctors tell you. There is hope in Jesus Christ our Lord and Savior. He is a mighty God that we serve. Amen.

Anita Chavez

In 2000, Anita Chavez was diagnosed with major depression and schizophrenia with psychosis. Her journey with mental illness lasted five long years, until God through His Grace delivered her. She is currently involved in disciplining women through various ministry efforts as she continues to seek a deeper relationship with Jesus Christ.

Contact: anitamchavez@gmail.com

A GHETTO KID LIKE ME

Aaron Thomas

"He also brought me up out of a horrible pit,
Out of the miry clay, and set my feet upon a rock, and established my steps.
He has put a new song in my mouth –
Praise to our God;
Many will see it and fear and will trust in the Lord."
– Psalm 40:2-3

I was a child unwanted, born in my mother's sin and iniquity. It was so bad that my mom was going to give me away. I was fatherless, black, and impoverished in typical inner-city black America during the sixties and seventies when folks were trying to figure out that people were people.

If you know anything about the inner city, then you know that you claim your street. I grew up in southwest Philadelphia, 111 East Minor Street. I watched pimps, players, women slayers - I saw how these men lived. They influenced me. I was a dope dealer at five-years-old. The boys in the hood were good to me, they taught me. I walked up the street to get milk at the corner store where I used to drop off packages. I didn't know what I was doing, but I knew it was how I made money.

My mom had five kids and no job but thought that everything was okay because she had "friends." She entrusted us to these "friends," two men who molested me and my brothers from the age of three to the age of eight, who put me in front of their little sister and told me to touch her here and touch her there. I became sexually perverse. I knew it was wrong but it felt good. I was twisted, angry, hurt. And I continued to do it because they paid me. Inside, I was confused. Did I like men? Was it okay for me to be with men? I was a teenager with twisted views of how to deal with women and life.

My anger grew as I became a stick up kid, a hustler, a player. At thirteen-years-old, kids can get little jobs, but I knew what the streets taught me: how to break into people's houses; how to steal; how to hustle; how to deal. I was the provider, but I lived a duplicitous life. In that horrible pit, I became pitiful. I didn't know who God was. I figured He didn't really have time for me or He would've never left me abandoned, homeless, and poor. I was the victim of a ghetto kid's life.

One day, I decided to become a drug dealer. I tried drugs and did drugs and sold drugs and pushed drugs and I ended up in prison. I went to prison for a long time (I'm not telling you stories of all the other times that I was arrested, incarcerated, and held for questioning). In prison I started reading the Bible, not because I wanted to serve God, but because He might help me get through prison. So I used God like a lot of us do. I called on Him in need but I didn't belong to Him. I read the Bible twenty or thirty times, up until the day the guards came and said you're about to get out of prison. I cried and told God I will not serve you anymore. I don't want to live the life that you have for me. I can't do it. I'm still interested in women, drugs, and alcohol. When I got out of prison, I continued the lifestyle.

During that time, I met a woman who belonged to God. On our first date we spent two and a half hours talking about God. I didn't know that God was in me, but I knew that God was in her and that scared me. I ran from her for four years. When I finally came back to her, we got married. I had to take a real hard look at myself. This woman had seen the evil in me, the dirt in me, but she also saw something else. So I made a decision to address my drug and alcohol addiction. I would travel to a Christian Men's Restoration Home in Houston to find out who this God was, to prove that he didn't care about a ghetto kid like me. I went out to Houston for a month. I stayed for nine months.

Needless to say, God got a hold of me. I became saved, but that was only the beginning. I thought, "I have this God thing down. I'm saved, sanctified, and filled with the Holy Ghost!" But

God goes, "No, no, no; that's just the beginning. You have to grow in faith, knowledge, understanding, godliness, and brotherly love." I was like, "I don't know how to do that." But God said, "I'll do it. I'll do it through you." And so He started to transform my life. And in that transformation He showed me things that I hadn't dealt with yet. I thought drugs and alcohol were my problem, but He said that integrity and character were my problem.

He took me to a class of post abortive fathers. In my sexual immorality, I had impregnated five different women. Whether by omission or commission I said nothing when they aborted my child. I didn't know that it was an issue until God introduced it to me. I said, "Wait a minute, God. I've been with you for a few years and you're trolling this up now?" God said, "I've got to get that pit up out of you." And that's what He did. He excavated the evil inside.

Salvation might be instantaneous, but sanctification is a process. I'm going through that process still. Me being here is a part of that process. God is revealing my immorality. "This is the thorn in your side," He says. "Since you were three, Satan has been messing with you." I said, "Why did you wait God?" He said, "My timing is perfect. I know who you are in Me. You aren't a womanizing, lying, double-minded criminal. You are who I say you are. I am the great I am. And Aaron, you are redeemed."

I am redeemed. I am restored, renewed, right, reconciled. I am a new creation in Jesus Christ, born again as a child. Today I stand before you seven years old in Jesus. I am a son of God, wonderfully and fearfully made. The world has told me lies. My mother lied to me; my family lied to me; the colour of my skin lied to me; my economic woes lied to me. Before I am a man, I am a Christian. Before I am an African-American, I am a Christian. Before I am a husband, I am a Christian. Before I am a father, I am a Christian. I am part of the great I Am, and I'm here to testify to the wonderful love and mercy of grace that God renews in me every day.

The battle wages on. I am a soldier in the Army of the Lord, here to fight for His name, His honour, and His glory. Life told me that I had no purpose. Life lied to me. I'm heir to a kingdom in heaven. When I'm done fighting, when I'm done testifying, and when He's done sanctifying, God will bring me home. I am his child. He pulled me up out of a horrible pit, out of the muck and the mire, and placed a song in my heart. Others will hear it. And they will come to trust in the Lord thy God. Amen.

Aaron D. Thomas

Born in Washington DC, Pastor Thomas originally lived just outside of Philadelphia, PA. Moving to New Mexico at the age of 12, Pastor Thomas attended New Mexico State University and Cross Christian Bible College where he received his degree. Pastor Thomas is fully charged by our Lord and Savior Jesus Christ to proclaim and defend His glorious gospel. Pastor Thomas and his wife Michelle have four children and four beautiful grandchildren.

Contact: peaceoutreachministry@yahoo.com

TOO BAD

Amanda Currier

"For I know the thoughts that I think toward you, says the Lord, thoughts of peace and not of evil, to give you a future and a hope."
– Jeremiah 29:11

As a child, I was the churchy girl. Squeaky clean. I loved going to church, it was fun. My mom said she never had to worry about me because I always made the right choice. But when I was 16-years-old I began dating a guy my parents didn't approve of. We fought, and I ended up quitting my family, quitting my church, and quitting God.

Three years later, I got pregnant. I decided that I wanted to keep the baby, but I was terrified to tell my boyfriend. I hid my pregnancy until the end of my first trimester. Ultimately, my boyfriend told me to get rid of it. He said abortion is not what it used to be. After hours of yelling and crying, it boiled down to him or the baby. I chose him.

I went to the clinic. The day went by in slow motion. I remember there was a lady outside saying, "Don't do it. We can help. We can find you a home." I started to walk toward her, but that's when the clinic escorts came and took me inside.

Once inside, fear and shame overwhelmed me. I began trembling. "They haven't called my name yet," I thought. "I can get up and go." That's when they called my name. They took me to the back to do an ultrasound to determine how far along I was. I couldn't look at the doctors or the ultrasound screen. I stared at the wall while tears burned inside my throat. They determined, yup, we can do a section abortion, and handed me a hospital gown. I was on auto pilot. I wasn't moving my own feet. A paralyzing fear gripped me. I wanted to tell the doctors and nurses, "No, wait, I've changed my mind!" I wanted to scream, "Stop!" But no words came out.

When I left the clinic, I looked for the lady outside. I was ready to tell her that I'd made a terrible mistake. Was there anything they could do to help me? But she was gone and so was all of my hope. I sat in my car and cried. I called my boyfriend to tell him it was done. I called him 14 times. There was no answer. As I drove home in silence I knew there was no way God would ever forgive me now. I became closed off and calloused. I was angry all the time, hateful especially to myself. Inside I was empty. I had nothing left, no hope.

Four months later, I got pregnant again. With no feelings left inside of me, I went back to the clinic.

Life spun downward fast after that. My boyfriend got hooked on cocaine. I wanted to try it but I'm an epileptic. I was worried that if I tried the cocaine I would go into a seizure and then I'd have to go to a doctor and everyone would know. So I looked for another escape route. I contemplated suicide constantly. It dominated my life. I never connected my suicidal feelings to the abortions. In fact, I denied that they had ever happened. In my mind the abortions were pretend. I hated myself, but I didn't know why.

After two years of suicidal thoughts, I got pregnant a third time. This time, I stood my ground. I was not going to abort my baby. My boyfriend grabbed a loaded 12-gauge shotgun and said he would kill himself if I didn't have an abortion. I wrestled the shotgun away. He grabbed his keys, and took off out of the door. That was the last time I ever saw him.

I called my parents, whom I had rarely spoken to in the last five years. I moved back in with them. I tried to piece my life together the best that I could. I got my own place, had my baby, started going to school. But life was still miserable. The only joy I found was in my son.

When my son was two-years-old, I met a man, a Christian. We started going to church on Wednesday nights. Those were our dates. Supper and then church - some of the best dates ever. And one of those nights, I gave my life to Christ. I realized that there *was* hope out there. It was trickling into my life because I had Jesus now. But I kept the abortions separate. In my mind those were too bad. I could not be forgiven for those.

When I confessed my abortions to my new boyfriend, he wrapped his arms around me and said, I still love you. But I did not hear his voice. I heard God's. Six months later he and I were married. We had another wonderful boy together.

Later, I discovered a friend of mine had experienced an abortion, too, and yet she felt God's forgiveness. I confessed mine to her and asked, "How? How can you feel God's forgiveness?" She said something that hit me like a ton of bricks. She said, "By telling God that I was too bad of a sinner, I was saying He didn't do enough on the cross to pay for my sins. What else would I have Him do?" I realized then that He took the sin of my abortion, too.

I got pregnant once more but had a miscarriage nine weeks along. The baby I miscarried and the second baby I had aborted were both the same age, nine weeks. I knew beyond a shadow of a doubt that my miscarried baby was in heaven.

Why didn't I think my aborted babies were? I began praying for forgiveness until I realized that I had it, that my children were safe in the arms of God. That is when the floodgates of hope just poured into my life.

I talked to my pastor. He directed me to a grief group where I met three other ladies who'd had abortions. We began a post-abortive Bible study. I watched Jesus change the lives of these three amazing women. Now, the four of us lead a post-abortive Bible study to show that there is hope after abortion. Jesus is determined to show us His love. He has a future for us. "For I know the plans I have for you, declares the Lord, plans to prosper you and not to harm you. Plans to give you hope and a future." Amen.

Amanda Currier

Amanda works with several women in a ministry called Ashes to Beauty with the mission of furthering post abortive healing through post abortion Bible studies. Amanda also works with youth from various churches sharing her message of hope. Amanda and her husband Gene have been married for 7 years and have 3 beautiful children.

Learn More: www.ashesbeauty.org
Contact: acurrier@ashesbeauty.org

FRAUD GUY

Luke Lowenfield

"Teach us to number our days that we may gain a heart of wisdom."
-Psalms 90:12

In college I was two separate people. I was going to church services on Sunday, the University fellowship on Tuesday nights, and leading a men's Bible study group during the week. In the evenings I made a mockery of it all. I was the fraud guy.

There was no way that these two lifestyles could coexist, and yet I was totally comfortable being one way to certain people and a different way to others. I wanted my mom and dad to know that I was on the straight and narrow. I wanted my brothers to look up to me. But I also wanted to enjoy all of the guilty pleasures that the world had to offer. I was so insecure that I wanted to be liked by everyone. I had a thousand voices in my head: "Who should I be? What should I be doing?" It was insanity. It was only a matter of time before that came to an end, right?

For me that time came after graduating college. I was traveling in Mexico studying Spanish. After a couple of weeks, I woke up with a really intense pain in my stomach. It got worse and worse throughout the day until I was crying and screaming. I had this sense that if I closed my eyes I wouldn't open them again, like shutting off your computer. I felt like my life was just going to fade out. I was taken to the hospital where a doctor diagnosed me with acute pancreatitis. Later, when I was stabilized and back in the States, a doctor reviewed my medical report. "I don't know exactly what happened here," he said, "but based on everything I'm reading in your chart, you shouldn't be alive." That was the wake-up call that got my attention.

Thank God I had people in my life to care for me. I was born and raised in the best family. I had a dad who was a devoted, fantastic leader, a mom who loved the Lord and dedicated all of her time to me and my three brothers, grandparents who prayed for me and had me over for sleepovers. I had it as good as it gets, all of the best influences, and yet I had broken their trust. They had no reason to be loving me as they did, but they kept coming back, praying for me, encouraging me. It didn't make any sense.

In that hospital, something completely inexplicable happened. It happened one night as I was alone in the hospital bed, completely broken, totally humbled, hopeless and helpless. There was no way that I was going to fix myself. There was no way that I was going to fix my relationships. There was no way that I was going to get right before God. Still, I prayed. I asked for help. That was all that came out of my mouth, "Help." And in that moment, God showed up. I didn't see Him, but it was like a breath of wind on the back of my neck. It was unlike anything I'd experienced before, unlike anything I've experienced since. I believe that when I left that hospital it was like when I left 23 years prior as a baby. I was a new creation. My mom was driving me home just as she had 23 years before.

I had done the Bible studies, I had memorized the scripture, but back then it was just a book. Now, I was learning things for the first time spiritually. It was like a treasure chest had been sitting there but I never knew the value of it. Once I opened it, I couldn't get enough. Here was the answer to all of those questions I had about who I was and what I was supposed to be doing with my life. I found glorious, precious truths. That was one of the biggest changes, the scripture. Another was the way that I viewed people.

Before the hospital, I wanted people to like me. But once I came out of the hospital, God showed me that I only needed to please Him. Jesus wasn't living for everyone else, he was listening to one voice. Some people hated Him. Some people felt threatened by Him. But others loved Him, and continue to love Him, because He obeyed the Father. Instead of trying to please others, I only needed to live for Him. In doing so, I enjoyed His renewal and His blessings. With the help of my family, I was spiritually maturing, learning what it was to live as a disciple of Christ.

Shortly after God brought me into this new life, I got married. My wife is the greatest gift that God has given me on this Earth. What He shows me through her is the unconditional nature of His love for me. It's not that I do everything right as a husband, but my wife entered into a covenant with me that she's never going to break. That's what God's love is like: "I've entered into a covenant with you. I promise you I'm never going to leave you. I'm never going to forsake you."

God also teaches me about His love through my two precious children. Those of us who are parents know that when you have a child, new depths of love open up in your heart. I think, "How could you love me like that, God? Who could I possibly be that you would love me unconditionally, forever? Because I'm never going to stop loving these boys you've given me. And that's how you love *me*?" I'm completely undeserving, but I can have security in God's love.

Before Christ, I valued all the wrong things. Everything centered around me. In Christ, I value what He values: relationships that are beautiful and wonderful as they are. And there's a future hope, something eternal that's greater than even the greatest of relationships that I experience on Earth. It's life with the King. I don't have to fear the end of my days, because the King has defeated death and promised me the fullness of joy forevermore. Lord, would you teach us to number our days that we may gain a heart of wisdom? Amen.

Luke Lowenfield

Luke is blessed with a loving wife, Stacey, and two sons named Parker Clay and Jackson Graham. Luke studied business administration at Washington and Lee University and law at the University of Texas at Austin. He says his purpose in the marketplace is to love and serve the Casa family in a way that encourages each member toward a deeper sense of purpose in his or her job.

A CROOKED PATH TO GOD

Linda Hall

*"But the wisdom that is from above is first pure,
then peaceable, gentle,
willing to yield, full of mercy and good fruits..."
– James 3:17*

If you saw me at 15-years-old, I probably looked like any other teenage girl, but on the inside I was mourning the loss of my parents. My mom died when I was 12-years-old, and my dad was diagnosed with terminal cancer shortly therafter. When my stepmom and I moved to California, I fell in love with the area, especially the San Gabriel Mountains. I used to stand in the school hallway and just stare out the window between classes. But I was lonely. My stepmom and I weren't close. I developed a deep craving for the love of a man, probably as a substitute for the great relationship I'd had with my father.

I was a good girl: I did my chores and homework, I went to church, and I worked a part-time job. Then I met my first love. I was so thrilled that this guy thought that I was pretty. We ladies can be so easily swayed by the attentions of a man.

He was the manager of this little restaurant where I worked. He was older than me by a couple of years and very handsome. The equation in my head went something like this: if he thinks I'm pretty, then maybe I am valuable. To my 16-year-old heart, that felt so good. Glenn was the answer to my emptiness.

Unfortunately, my stepmom didn't see it that way. Glenn was Japanese. She called him a heathen Buddhist. It didn't help at all when I explained, "No, no, he's not Buddhist. He doesn't go to church at all." That night, she gave me an ultimatum. Either I stop dating Glenn or I move out. (For any parents reading this, when you give your kids an ultimatum, be prepared for them to make the worst choice.) For me, this was a no brainer; her or him, really? I packed everything in my old car and drove to work that night, homeless.

I asked a 16-year-old work friend if she had any idea where I could stay that night. At that point, I was gleaning wisdom from other 16-year-olds. Cindy said, "You can come live with me and my parents." I thought that was really nice of her. In fact, Cindy's family treated me a whole lot better than my own Christian family despite the fact that they didn't go to church at all. I'm not even sure they believed in God. That was the beginning of my turn from the Lord because, you see, my stepmom was a church-going woman, very "Christian" by her own profession. I think a lot of people who are hurt by someone in their church turn away from God. Maybe I just wanted an excuse to do anything I liked. Who better to run my life than me?

What followed was a long period of challenging years far from God. When my parents were alive, they were strict. There were a lot of no's, and young Linda did not like no. No profanity, no dancing, no kissing on TV, and on and on. But on my own, there were suddenly no rules. I felt like I had been raised in a shoebox with the lid firmly taped down and then one day, that lid was gone. I looked out, saw this great big exciting world, and thought, "Yippee!"

Doing whatever I wanted definitely had its consequences. I managed to finish high school, but just before I graduated, I got pregnant. My boyfriend and I got married, but shortly thereafter he got inducted into the army and was deployed to Vietnam. He didn't return until our daughter Stacy was nine-months-old. I thought, "This is going to be cool, like Leave it to Beaver." It wasn't at all like Leave it to Beaver. The reality was that our relationship was based on his physical attraction to me and my desire to be loved. We didn't have any common goals or interests. I wanted to play house and he wanted to numb the emotional wounds of war with his army buddies. Our relationship ended in divorce when Stacy was three-years-old. That would've been a great time for me to evaluate what went wrong and seek out help, but that's not what I did. Instead I got busy, because that's what I do best. I put my shoulder to the grindstone and pushed forward.

A few years later, I met a man I should never have been involved with. I was an adult, I knew better, but I deluded myself with excuses. We eventually got married and had a son, Casey. This relationship that started out on the wrong foot went downhill quickly when my husband became a drug addict. At the time, I was ignorant about drugs, but over the next seven years, I got my M.B.A. in dysfunctional living. My husband's drug of choice was crack cocaine. Our life became surreal. I was caught in a whirlwind of pathological lying, cheating, stealing, several arrests, family conflict, and total exhaustion. To deal with all of this chaos in my life, I developed my own co-dependency: I made excuses for him. I replaced the things he sold for drugs. I reported the cars he traded for drugs as stolen. I kept all of our dirty secrets from everyone.

Throughout this time, I drifted in and out of church. I was raised in the church, I was supposed to go to church, it was muscle memory. Once I had kids, I felt obligated to take them to church, too, but neither of my husbands had any interest, so most Sundays we did other stuff. I wasn't connected in the body of Christ, so when I missed service, nobody missed me.

When our son was four-years-old, I was on call with a helpline counselor trying to get my husband into yet another detox facility after a weekend of freebasing crack. The helpline counselor asked me what I was doing for myself and my kids and I quickly reminded her that I was calling for my husband, not myself. But she persisted. She asked me if his addiction had a negative impact on me or my kids. "Are you kidding me?" I said, incredulously. I conjured a laundry list of all of the terrible things we'd lived through. And then it hit me, the reality of my life. I knew I had to get out. After a lot of pain and suffering, my husband and I divorced. I was a single parent again. I wanted a life that had more meaning, that was more consistent with my profession of faith as a Christian. I was on a crooked path back to God.

The Bible tells us that we're not supposed to be unequally yoked, that believers shouldn't marry unbelievers, and I had intentionally disregarded that heavenly wisdom twice. I'm a slow learner, but I finally got it. I prayed that God would give me one more chance to do it right, and He answered that prayer in my husband Bob. When we met, we were both prodigal children, stumbling our way to God from different places. God has been faithful to us.

However, God wasn't quite done with me yet. I call it God hitting me upside the head with a 2x4. At the time, I was a successful executive with a large organization. About seven hundred people reported under me. In truth, it was work that helped maintain my sanity through my second marriage. I poured myself into my job like a bonafide workaholic, so God used a demotion to get my attention. I was shaken to the core. Then I thought, "What if God is letting this happen to me for a reason?" Between meetings with my bosses, I sat at my office desk and for the first time in my life, I submitted. "God, if this is from you," I prayed, "then I'm okay with it." And I actually meant it. Immediately I felt God's presence and peace. It was amazing.

I still got demoted. The new job was much less stressful and demanded a lot less time. Now I had time for God. I began studying the Bible. I was surprised that it was actually interesting, exciting, and practical. Going to church stopped being this childhood guilt-driven routine, and instead became a vital part of my life. And praying was no longer a big struggle for me. Now it was an ongoing conversation with God.

I've found great joy in serving in a single-parent ministry. I truly love these parents and their kids. I get what they're going through because I've walked in those shoes. Now we walk together, praising God for his loving mercy. I've sinned against God and others, and only God can rewrite that history. He calls me His friend and saint, and He lets me participate in His kingdom work. If you haven't tapped into the mercies God wants to shower on you, you're missing out on the best part, you really are. I stand here today totally dependent on God and loving it. Amen.

Linda Hall

Linda describes her history as "a checkered past"! But, she is quick to add that God was faithful to forgive her even though she had not been faithful to Him. By sharing some of the details of her struggles in early childhood which led to poor decisions later in life, Linda has seen others find understanding and hope through her story. If you lost parents at an early age, have had multiple broken relationships, been a single parent, dealt with drug addiction in a loved one or have lost an important position in business....you might find some common ground with Linda. As Linda says, "God took the lemons of my life and made lemonade!"

THE OCCULT

Barbara Reeves

"for I was hungry and you gave Me food; I was thirsty and you gave Me drink; I was a stranger and you took Me in; I was naked and you clothed Me; I was sick and you visited Me; I was in prison and you came to Me."
– Matthew 25:35-36

I received an ouija board for my birthday one year, and by the time I was 12-years-old, I was hooked. I entered into a life of the occult: ouija board, tarot cards, astrology, séances. My friends and I would practice levitation and other witchcraft in an attempt to gain supernatural knowledge. I thought, "I'm not doing anything *wrong*. God sends out power surges into the universe and if I have the sensitivity, I can tap right into his energy. And anyway, Jesus is far away. He doesn't care what I'm doing."

Over the years – throughout high school and college and medical school – I was still hooked on the occult. By the time I became a family practitioner, was married and had four beautiful children, I was not happy. I should have been happy by the world's standards: I was successful.

Instead, I was depressed. I was trying to find answers through these secret practices, but nothing was working. I was angry all of the time. I would come home from work stressed out and imagine picking up my kids by the scruff of their necks and slamming them into the wall. I was out of control in private, but in public, I was really nice. I sat through church on Sundays - a pew warmer - and then I would go back home, back to being unhappy.

It was then that I met a patient who was a former prostitute and drug addict, gloriously saved and delivered. She was super sweet, free-talking about Jesus like He was her best friend. I thought Jesus was far away and only worked through mysterious deeds. I thought I could access Him through the ouija board and tarot cards, but when I would get a response, the answers were confusing. And here was this woman who had an intimate relationship with Jesus - how? I made her come see me every two weeks for follow-up treatment. She said, "Gosh, I sure am sick a lot," but I just wanted to know, "What did Jesus do for you this time?"

A few months later, the Family Practice Department held our annual Christmas luncheon. One of the residents, a Christian, asked me out of the blue, "Do you think that the marriage feast of the lamb is going to be a sit down dinner or a buffet?" I said, "Ugh! Who would marry a lamb?

What are you talking about?" She said, "You know, after the Rapture." What the heck? I'd certainly never read this in the Bible. She looked concerned. "Barb," she said, "if you died today, would you go to Heaven?" I felt a huge hand push down on my right shoulder, and I knew it was God pushing me down toward Hell. I was really scared. I flubbed out some answer, like, "I try to be a good person," but that wasn't true at all. I didn't try to be a good person, I just tried not to get in trouble. She looked up, like she was listening. I thought, "Oh, great! I'm going to Hell and the only person who can help me is hearing voices." Then she said, "You need to go to a Christian bookstore right now and buy Frank Peretti's novel, *This Present Darkness*."

As soon as the luncheon was over, I rushed out to buy the book, raced home, and read from cover to cover. I told my poor husband, "Shut up. Don't bother me. Watch the kids, feed them, and put them to bed. I'm reading this book." It was the story of a woman about my age - I was 37 at the time - who was into the occult. Jesus gloriously saved her. It clearly spelled out the Gospel message.

At 4 a.m., I read the last page, closed the book, and knelt by my bed. I turned out the lights because I didn't want anybody to see me praying. I said, "Jesus, I've ignored you my whole life. If you will forgive me, then I'm yours. I'll follow you for the rest of my life. I'm going to picture myself jumping off of a cliff into your arms. If you don't catch me, I'm doomed." I felt washed clean. I knew that He had said yes, that I was free and forgiven and on the right road.

The next day, I returned to the Christian bookstore and bought a Bible. The cashier told me that the day previous I had yelled at her, saying, "Give me this book!" Okay. It was time to read the Bible. Soon after, the attacks of rage toward my kids and others disappeared, praise God. I was so happy, so grateful.

I was still serving patients from all walks of life, indigent patients who slipped through the cracks. Many wouldn't return for follow-up treatment because they couldn't afford a second visit. I thought, "Somebody needs to start a free clinic." It wasn't until later that I realized that somebody was *me*. My pastor said, "If you feel the need for a ministry, it might be that God's telling you to start it." So I started Harvest Medical Ministry, a free Christian clinic. Every patient was individually prayed for as part of their treatment. We traveled from church to church in an old RV. Four churches welcomed us in and let us use their space.

One day, a pastor with whom we partnered called and said, "Barb, you're not going to be able to come this week. We have to sell the church." I hung up and thought, "Oh goodness! Lord, please let somebody buy that church who will accept our free clinic." In my heart, I felt the Lord say, "You buy it." Now, doctors don't buy buildings. They rent them. But this church was strategically located in the center of the city and I wanted it. I called the pastor back and he said, "I knew it! I didn't even hire a realtor. The Lord told me you were going to buy it."

Of course, I didn't have the money. I made appointments at a couple of banks, but they wanted to know how I would repay the loan. "How much do you expect to make per month from your patients," they asked, and I answered, "Nothing." Really? I hope that works for you. After a couple of months, I wasn't getting anywhere. I cried out to the Lord, "I don't know what to do. How am I going to buy this building?" I was sitting at my husband's rolltop desk. The Lord told me, "Open the desk and look in the drawer." Inside, there was a savings policy that my husband had started back in 1979. Since then, he had suffered multiple sclerosis, was bedridden and demented, unaware of this paperwork. It was enough money to pay cash for the building.

13 years into the ministry, we've served over 8,000 patients. We're a regular family practice, but we also serve the homeless and ex-cons and anybody else that falls through the cracks, anybody that needs help. We present the Gospel

to everyone and pray with each patient, intercede for them. We've had wonderful stories of healing and delivery. And God has always supernaturally supplied over the years. I'm so grateful to the Lord for saving me, turning me from a horrible path onto the solid rock of Jesus. Amen.

Barbara Reeves

Barbara Reeves has practiced medicine in El Paso , TX for 30 years and is boarded in family medicine. Reeves has been recognized by the El Paso Commission of Women for her work with the Harvest Medical Ministry Clinic, a volunteer-based clinic.

THE LEPER

Ann Edenfield Sweet

"Assuredly, I say to you, inasmuch as you did it to one of the least of these My brethren, you did it to Me."
– Matthew 25:40

When I got a job with Continental Airlines, I thought, wow, I get to see the world. And it was in seeing the world that I met a pilot. We started a life together, married, and had four beautiful boys. Everything was perfect. I had a perfect marriage, a perfect family. That's when I got the phone call that would change my life forever.

My husband had been arrested, handcuffed in front of our real estate office and hauled off to the local jail. Overnight I was thrown into a world that was entirely foreign to me. My husband signed a 15-year plea agreement to conspiracy to import drugs. He ended up at La Tuna Federal prison near El Paso, TX leaving me penniless. In fact, I ended up with a three-and-a-half million dollar IRS lien that lasted for 16 years. My baby was on oxygen at the time and I couldn't even pay for his oxygen.

We'd been members of our church for 12 years, but not one person called. Without God, I guarantee I wouldn't be here today. But God spoke to me, introduced me to a pastor who welcomed me into a new church. He touched my hand and prayed with me and for me. This pastor had the courage to hire me as the church's youth director. We started with eight kids and in five years we had over 250 youth in the program. I guarantee you I was the most blessed person of all. My boys and I just loved it. I only made $800 per month, but I was the richest person around.

Six years into his sentence, my husband called and said that he was coming home. I ran in to tell the pastor, whom I had worked with for almost two years, the news. In front of the whole staff he said, "Well, I can no longer be your pastor." I thought it was a joke. "I'm a leper again," I thought. "It doesn't matter that I'm the youth director. I'm an outcast."

At the time, I was working on a book called "Family Arrested" about how to survive the incarceration of a loved one. As an airline attendant, I'd flown all over the world, experienced foreign countries, but *prison*? That was a foreign world I couldn't comprehend. But it took years for someone to publish my book. In the meantime, I met the New Mexico Prison Fellowship Director. I was like, I know what you want me to do God! You want me to take my work as a youth director to the families of prisoners so that we may all be welcomed into the church.

I got a $3,000 grant for a three-month program. We called it the Wings Ministry. Eventually we were invited into the prisons and I thought, "This is the best of all, to gather the inmates and their wives and parents and children and grandchildren for a party." We sang and dramatized scripture. We did crafts and activities, ate together and played games. It was truly God's party. Inmates said, "This is the first time I've held my loved one's hand and prayed with them."

I realized then that God had uniquely qualified me. I had grown up in one of those Leave It to Beaver families: four kids, parents who loved each other, church every Sunday. I was involved in church and school as the leader of the Luther League, student council president, and homecoming queen. God grew me, he taught me as a young child in the church how to be a leader. He walked me through my life in order to reach out to these families. That's why I started a second program called "Wings for LIFE." We want to give people wings to fly for the rest of their lives, life skills imparted through education. God uses me and my experiences, because no employers wanted to hire someone associated with a three-and-a-half million dollar IRS lien and a husband in prison.

"Wings for LIFE" is in ninteen states now. It's always moving when I meet people at the lowest point in their lives, because I've been there. I've been the leper. I was the one to tell my children no, they couldn't play with the neighbors next door; no, they weren't invited to the birthday party. Because I've lived it, I can reach out and help. I feel honored to lead this ministry, for as scripture tells us in Matthew 25:40, "I tell you, just as you did to one of the least of these who are members of my family, you did it to me." Amen.

Ann Edenfield-Sweet

Ann is an internationally recognized motivational keynote speaker, popular TV and radio show guest, and frequent leader of workshops and trainings at national and international conferences. In 1995 Ann founded the Wings Ministry, a program for family members of inmates. Wings Parties have been held in prisons and/or communities in fifteen states, India, and Kenya. Ann also founded Wings second program, Wings for L.I.F.E. - Life-skills Imparted to Families through Education, which is an empowerment/ support group for the entire family that builds Search Institute's® 40 Developmental Assets,® and offers support and education for children, parents/caregivers, and returning citizens.

Learn More: www.wingsforlifeinternational.org

PHYSICS OF MIRACLES

Steve Cunningham

"Eye has not seen, nor ear heard,
Nor have entered into the heart of man
The things which God has prepared for those who love Him."
– 1 Corinthians 2:9

I am a scientist with a PhD in Theoretical Solid State Physics. I completed six years in post-doctoral studies, served as a Visiting Associate at Caltech, wrote over 50 articles that have been published in scientific journals, and worked for Boeing in the spacecraft design business. I tell you this to try to convince you that I really am a scientist. Every now and then, I have to convince myself that I am a scientist, that I am trained to be skeptical about things that I observe. Because, you see, I believe in miracles.

I grew up in a Christian home. I professed my faith in Jesus and was baptized at the age of 12-years-old. However, my family went to a church that believed the Bible was great literature, but not literally true. The miracles in the Bible didn't really happen as described, but were hyperbole to emphasize the writer's story. For example, Jesus didn't actually provide food for 5,000 men, but rather made them all feel guilty so that they shared the food that each was hiding. Moses didn't actually split the Red Sea; a strong wind blew the water of a shallow lake. As a consequence, my faith in God was weak when I entered college.

I have a vivid memory of walking across campus to a physics class at age 19, having a conversation with "God." I told him, "I don't believe in a God that sits on a throne in a white robe. I don't believe in a God who cares about how I live or what I do. I reject you as a concept. I'm going to figure out how to live for myself." Fortunately, lightening did not strike me dead!

For 10 years, I wandered from one religion to another in pursuit of the meaning of life. I studied the Eastern religions for several years and then later switched to Christian Science. Next I tried a traditional Christian church, but couldn't get past the fact that the church was full of hypocrites. I joined a Unitarian church, but left when the local pastor declared that there was no God. In hindsight, I see that I was trying to fill a void in my life, a void that I didn't realize was there and wouldn't have been able to label as such.

Things changed dramatically at age 29. At that time, my brother invited me to attend a small church in California, where a visiting radio personality was giving a service. After he finished speaking, he called for anyone with a prayer request to come forward. I was sitting in the 6th row near the central aisle, observing in full analytic mode. The speaker prayed for several people down the row. When he got to an elderly lady, she said she wanted prayer for her eyes. He offered a short prayer, maybe 20 seconds, and moved on to the next person. But then he stopped short, because this woman declared that she could see. At that, the gathering came apart.

Later I learned that this woman was a longtime member of that church. Every one knew her, and knew that she was blind, and had been for several years. The visiting speaker had no prior connection to her. So what I know with certainty is: before the prayer she was blind, and after the prayer she could see. Witnessing an instantaneous miracle changed my worldview. As a scientist, I am trained to observe the physical world and explain how it works. Here, I witnessed a change in the physical world that came about by an unobserveable force. This event convinced me (as no amount of discussion could) that there is a supernatural power that can enter this world and effect change. Shortly thereafter, I recommitted my life to Jesus. I was convinced that the Bible was the way to learn more about this supernatural power.

Since then, I have witnessed other miracles.

My favorite is Rex. At two-years-old, Rex fell into a swimming pool and drowned. 34-minutes elapsed between discovering his body and doctors re-starting his heart in the hospital. Prayer requests went out to a number of people and to the local Christian TV station. The doctor, who happened to be our Pediatrician and a member of our Sunday school class, examined Rex and gave him a coma score of 3, which meant there was no chance of recovery without brain injury. After consultation, the decision was made to discontinue doctors' heroic life-saving efforts. Rex was declared dead at 9:30 p.m. Awake at 3:00 a.m. and longing for closure, the mother decided to return to the hospital to say goodbye to her son. She held Rex in her arms, and that's when she detected warmth and motion. Amidst joy and frantic activity in the hospital, Rex's recovery began. Today, he is 33-years-old and perfectly healthy.

Then there's Laura, a girl of 12 who was suffering from scoliosis of the spine. The doctor told her parents that if the disease continued along its trend, Laura would need a body cast until her bones stopped growing. The parents asked our small Bible study group to come into their home and pray for Laura, something we infrequently did. We met, read some scripture to bolster our faith, and then prayed. At the end of the meeting, none of us sensed that anything had changed, but a month later, when Laura went in for a check-up, the doctor called everyone into his office. He mounted a series of X-rays from the past three-and-a-half years. It was obvious to everyone the progression of the disease: the first six X-rays showed a worsening of the curvature of the spine. The seventh X-ray was completely normal. The doctor had no explanation for it. What I know is, Laura needed a body cast, but after directed prayer, she was healed.

For me, miracles are a sign that point to a supernatural God who is intimately involved in our lives, a God who is revealed to us both in his creation and by the wisdom in the Bible. Miracles aid us in believing in Jesus. I really like what E. Stanley Jones wrote about miracles: "I believe in miracle, but not too much miracle... Just enough miracle to let us know He his here…lest we depend on it when we should depend on our own initiative and on His orderly processes for our development."

I am convinced that it is "unscientific" to deny the existence of miracles. The evidence of supernatural events is all around us, often so subtle that it appears to be circumstantial. Miracles defy the natural laws of physics; the real world is more than just what we can observe. As a scientist, trained to be skeptical, I know that there is a living God behind those miracles. Amen.

Stephen L. Cunningham

Steve has been trained as a scientist with a PhD in Theoretical Solid State Physics. He has written over 50 articles published in scientific journals. In 1984 he was one of 4 Hughes engineers selected to fly on the Space Shuttle, but due to the Challenger accident in 1986 that killed one of the Hughes Payload Specialists, the program was discontinued and Steve never flew. He currently works at Boeing Space and Information Services.

SHINE ON

Gabriel Moore

"The people who walked in darkness
Have seen a great light;
Those who dwelt in the land of the shadow of death,
Upon them a light has shined."
– Isaiah 9:2

I vividly remember driving around my neighborhood in my stepfather's Buick Regal. It was nighttime. I was eight-years-old. When a gentleman approached the passenger window, we stopped. I could barely see out of the window. The stranger handed me money. My stepfather gave me the nod, so I counted the bills, but I was just learning how to count money. "Twenty, forty, sixty-five," I said. "No, you got it wrong, son," he said. "Twenty, forty, sixty, eighty." I counted two hundred dollars. My stepdad told me good job. Now I could get a new winter coat. He handed me a white bag that I passed to the guy in the window. Then we drove off to buy my winter coat.

This moment is very important to me now, but I didn't understand it then. I thought my father was doing what a father does. He teaches his child how to count money. I never told my mom - could not tell my mom. I didn't even tell her three weeks later when she held me in front of the television, crying as we watched my stepfather duck into a police car. It was one of the biggest drug busts in Fort Worth, Texas history. 22 federal indictments. My stepfather served 17 years in the penitentiary.

It was a struggle growing up. My mom, a beautiful woman who worked three jobs, taught me hardwork, dedication, patience, and endurance. Three boys, three girls. Six different attitudes from six different kids, and only one mom? She was determined to raise men and women who would seek after the Lord. "You know, Gabriel," she'd say, "the way you're living your life is only a phase. God is going to use you." And I'd say, "Ah, whatever ma. You don't know what you're talking about. May I have the keys, please?" She'd repeat herself: "Watch the company that you keep. This is only a phase. You're powerful. I love you. God loves you." And I would go about my way because I thought that I was cool. My mom did everything that she could for me, but the streets, the music, the videos, they shot straight to my soul and changed my character.

One night when I was in eighth grade, I got a call. My friend said, "Gabe, wake up, man. Ro's been shot. Man, they just shot my brother. The

Crips. A gang fight." 17-years-old and shot twice in the head. His death rocked my life. The next day at school a teacher told me that I had to do something to get it out. I had to talk. I had to write. I was like, no, I don't plan on doing anything. And she asked, "Have you written poetry before?" I thought, "Poetry? Poetry is for suckers." I didn't know anything about Edgar Allan Poe, Langston Hughes, Maya Angelou. Didn't know anything about anything. She made me write a poem, a requiem, which means song for the dead. As a freshman in high school that was my first poem. And I never wrote a poem again until I was a freshman in college.

By God's grace, I came to know Jesus Christ as my Lord and Savior while in college. I was like, "God, maybe my Mom was right. Maybe You are going to do something with me. Let's go." I started to write spoken word poetry about how good God is. Spoken word poetry is rap, it's music. The only people who have realized the influence of music are corporations like Coca Cola and Chrysler. But many churches look down on that. For me, spoken word is a tool that I use to share the Gospel. It does not make me. It's my relationship with God through Jesus Christ, reflected in my writing like the moon reflects the sun. Everywhere I go, I minister through spoken word.

At performances the kids are like, "God, I want to know you. I want to know more about you."

Sometimes, the average audience members are older, so I cut out the slang and add the "g" to the end of my "-ing" words. No matter who is listening, I want to glorify God. I just happen to do it in rap form. Metaphor. It's the same Gospel, the same God, just different mediums. I think about David in Psalms, "Because your loving kindness is better than life, my lips will glorify You." I feel the same way. I think David was a pretty cool poet, by the way.

I recently got a chance to thank the teacher who encouraged me to write. She remembered me, how stubborn I was. She made sure she told me that. And I said, "You have no idea!" I signed one of my books to her, and she cried.

This is the verdict. The light has come into this world. But men love darkness rather than light because their deeds are evil. I refuse to be one of those people, so when this light came on, when this light came on, I reflected it, because this light, this light is the potential home in each of us. And I chilled on the highest hill that I could climb to shine for those with no power. Still looking for the light. Shine on. Amen.

Gabriel Moore

Gabriel Moore's gift of evangelism through poetry is an art form developed through both the struggle growing up and through the grace of coming to know the Lord. His passion is commonly simple. Strive to live out the Gospel daily, cherish the Word of God, and teach others to do the same.

Contact: gxm013@yahoo.com

BROKEN HOME

Amber Tracy

"Trust in the Lord with all your heart
and lean not on your own understanding.
In all your ways acknowledge Him,
and He shall direct your paths."
-Proverbs 3:5-6

As a little girl, I always wanted to spend time with my grandma. She gave me the attention and affection that I craved. After school I would go home, lean out the window, and watch for her car in the driveway. We spent every evening together since my mom was an alcoholic and my dad was a workaholic.

I was eight-years-old when my mom went into a coma for three weeks due to alcohol. The doctors told us that she wasn't going to live. They said, "Her pancreas completely shut down. Nobody survives this." The news didn't really affect me because I had my grandma. She was my mom. I clung to her like never before. Then, a miracle. My mom woke up. Nobody knew how or why. When the doctors sent my mom home they told her, "You won't make it if you drink alcohol." So my mom underwent a life change: she started doing pain pills. For two years she was addicted to pills, up until my grandmother passed away which led to a newfound cocaine addiction.

Without my grandma, I had to face the broken home that I'd run from, a home filled with fighting, yelling, and now my mom's cocaine addiction. That's when I turned to sports. My teammates provided the love that I missed from my grandma. At sports practice, I didn't have to worry about what was going on at home. I could focus on the game. I could take my anger out on the competition and leave it there on the court. I fell in love with basketball. I would go to practice after school and then practice after practice so that I wouldn't have to go back home.

This whole time I was questioning God. To me, God was a Sunday thing because every Sunday my dad would take me to Catholic church and then breakfast. I felt like I couldn't say "God" outside of church. When we stopped going to church, I didn't think about God again until my sophomore year of high school.

I was so lost then, so alone, that I contemplated suicide for months. God probably laughed at me. He was like, "You have this suicide planned out, but I have something greater for you." That's when He brought my nephew into the world. I remember when he was born, I was the last person to hold him. He grabbed my pinky and wouldn't let go. The nurse was like, "Hey, we've got to weigh him," and I was like, "Good luck." I tried to stay out of their way but he just held onto my pinky the whole time. Talk about a miracle! It was then that I decided this boy would have an amazing childhood, despite our broken home. I was no longer living for myself. I wanted to be a role model for my nephew. This glimpse of faith allowed me to start questioning God again. I visited different churches around the city, trying to find the best place to raise my nephew in God.

A Baptist church invited me to a retreat where I met Addison Road, the host. She came from a broken home, too, and I found my story in her. It was the first time in my life that I heard, "It's not about religion, it's about a relationship." God was waiting with open arms to give me all the love I ever wanted. I accepted Christ into my heart, and I wish I could say it was all rainbows and butterflies from then on, but when I came back home, nothing really changed. I still felt lost and hopeless, but now I had responsibilities. I was like, "Great. I can't mess up for all of us."

I turned down a couple of sports scholarships to stay home and take care of my nephew. I decided that I was done with sports. God laughed at me again and said, "Yeah, right." Sure enough, a couple of my high school friends invited me to try out for the university softball team. I thought, "What? I don't even like softball. I like basketball.

But whatever, I'll go." There were 50 girls who tried out. I was the only one that made the team. Everyone was so excited, but like everything else that I'd been through, I just wanted to run from it. I started as a practice player and then had opportunities to be on the field.

In my sophomore year of college, a couple of teammates wanted to start a Fellowship for Christian Athletes. They asked me to help and I was like, "I'm all in. It sounds awesome. It's where God and sports come together!" I remembered Addison Road and thought, "Maybe this is my new start." I started going to sports camps. I became a huddle leader, guiding high school athletes to Christ. Between my coaches and my teammates and these high school girls, I had a chance to actually see Christ working in my life for the first time.

Then God gave me a vision. Maybe I could reach other kids who played sports in order to escape home. After all, we didn't have a Fellowship for Christian Athletes where I was from. God gave me a vision to not only spread FCA throughout my city, but the entire state. I wanted to be *that person* for kids, that person I wish I'd had when I was younger, someone to be the hands and feet of Christ. God told me, "You already are." It's Him who gives me the strength to repair this broken home. "Trust in the Lord with all your heart and lean not on your own understanding. In all your ways acknowledge Him and He shall direct your paths." Amen.

Amber Tracy

Amber completed her bachelors degree in Exercise Science at the University of New Mexico and is now in the school of medicine at UNM studying occupational therapy. She is actively involved in the Fellowship of Christian Athletes using her platform as an athlete to reach youth for Christ.

Contact: atracy@salud.unm.edu

MARKETPLACE AND MISSIONS

AJ Jackson

The poor will never cease from the land;
therefore I command you, saying,
"You shall open your hand wide to your brother,
to your poor and your needy in your land."
– Deuteronomy 15:11

A young boy lived in a fishing village. From time to time, he would go down to the harbour where the fishing boats docked with their daily catch. The fishermen would discard the stray starfish from their nets onto the shore, and the little boy would walk along the beach, picking up starfish and throwing them back into the water. One of the fishermen yelled, "Kid, what are you doing? We throw hundreds of starfish on the beach. You can't save them all. It doesn't matter." The little boy picked up another starfish, threw it into the water, and said, "Well, it matters to that one."

A pastor in South America told me this story back in 2006. I had just earned a business degree and was gearing up to be a full-blown real estate business dude. Make money. Party. Chase girls. But I wasn't happy. I knew from my Christian upbringing that the void could only be filled by God, and so I attended a church service. Out of the hundreds of people there, the pastor preached to me. I rededicated my life to the Lord right then, saying, "Hey, God? I want to be used by you. Tell me to do something and I'll do it." A couple of months later, my parents invited me on a trip to South America. They work with a ministry called Faith Comes By Hearing, so it was a chance to do God's work. I said, "That sounds like a pretty good opportunity."

In South America, I met Pastor Javier and we hit it off, became friends. Near the end of the trip, he pulled me aside. It was like the whole room went silent. He said, "The Lord wants you to be in business and ministry. The two will be one, like a marriage. You will work with orphans and widows, the poor and the displaced." I knew that the Lord was speaking through him, so I was stoked. I went home and prayed, "Okay God, what does this mean?" He answered me with Deuteronomy 15:11.

I continued to pray for direction while simultaneously starting my own real estate company. That's when a buddy of mine approached me and said, "Hey dude, you should go to Thailand. There's a lot of need there." In the back of my mind I was like, "Duh! There's need everywhere." But I bought some backpacks, Googled some stuff, and said, "Let's do this."

Our local contact was a pastor named Manat, a schoolteacher. We're 23-years-old, 24-years-old, and he was my dad's age, just really old. He was also great. We explained to him that we didn't know what we were doing, we just knew that God wanted us in Thailand. Pastor Manat traveled with us all over the country, to schools and villages, to his friends' houses and churches and orphanages, asking, "Is this it?" We'd pray and pray, but it never felt right.

Now, Pastor Manat didn't speak the greatest English. Instead of yes, he said "can"; instead of no, he said "cannot". We'd be at a little Thai restaurant that served soup with a chicken foot sticking out of it. Pastor Manat would say, "Can," as in, yes, you can eat that. But I was like, "Cannot." I did not want to eat that! It continued this way for two weeks, traveling together and eating together, but we hadn't yet found our calling. Finally, we traveled northwest of Thailand, south of Chiang Mai, where Pastor Manat introduced us to Mae La refugee camp. It opened in 1984, when I was only two-years-old. 50,000 refugees from Burma or Myanmar lived there, but we had never heard of it. I was thinking, "This is it. This is why God brought us here!" But after a day at the camp: nothing. I was frustrated, so when Pastor Manat suggested visiting Metawa, an area further north, I was like, "Okay, fine, but we're leaving after that."

In Metawa, we stumbled across a group of 10 families living in bamboo huts. No running water, no electricity. "Manat," we asked, "what's up with these people?" He said, "Same, same." The same from Mae La camp: Burma, refugees. As we're walking through the village, God said, "This is why I brought you here. These are the people with whom you're supposed to work." I told Pastor Manat, "I don't know how in the world we're going to do this - I don't even know what we're going to do - but God told me this is where we're supposed to be, with these people, these kids. Do you know of somebody that can help us out?" And he said, "Two weeks before you arrived, God told me to quit my job as a teacher. Now I know why. God wants me to work with you."

How was it going to work? How were we going to help these people if I was on the other side of the world and Pastor Manat could barely speak English? I was so overwhelmed. He said, "I know a story. There's this little boy who used to go down to the harbour where the fishermen bring their boats." He told me the same story that the pastor in South America had told me. Talk about confirmation! Seven years later, my real estate investment company and ministry are one, like a marriage; the purpose of my business is to serve the ministry by helping to fund Forgotten Foundation projects. The Forgotten Foundation has been working on the border of Thailand and

Burma since 2008 with the goal of bringing the Gospel, relief, safety, community, education and love to the Karen people and other ethnic minorities who have escaped the war in Burma. Manat is still working for us in Thailand, where he employs a team of nine people. Amen.

AJ Jackson

AJ Jackson is married to Katrina, who he says is his beautiful partner and a true gift from God. They run a real estate investment company together in which the goal is to use profits to help fund Forgotten projects and other Kingdom works. Most recently AJ was honored in his community as one of the top business leaders under 40 years old.

Learn More: www.forgottenfoundation.com

FROM GENESIS TO REVELATION

Terence Chatmon

"Therefore, leaving the discussion of the elementary principles of Christ, let us go on to perfection, not laying again the foundation of repentance from dead works and of faith toward God"
– Hebrews 6:1

To be quite candid with you, I'm not supposed to be here today. At 6-weeks-old, my father inadvertently left me in a basket behind the rear wheel of a car. Walking into the house, he suddenly turned as the car was inches away from crushing me, and yelled, "Stop!" He saved my life. Six months later, I stood in my crib, eating paint off of the wall. In the old days, paint had lead in it, and I got lead poisoning. The doctor said, "Your son will probably not make it through the night." But I had parents who prayed for me.

My mother was the spiritual leader in our home, the epitome of love. She taught us that every life has its own eccentric value, down to the stray cats she took in. My father was the breadwinner, the Union president for 45 years. "Terence," he once said, "I never had a strike on my watch. I treated the executive just as I did the janitor." He taught us that we are not better than anyone else, but we are not inferior to anyone either.

You see, I grew up in Chicago, Illinois - a segregated city, a city that blocked Martin Luther King, Jr. from continuing his march. Not Alabama. Not the South. *Chicago*. It was so bad that in eighth grade, the teachers would guide my brother and I out of the back door 15 minutes before school let out so that we could run home. Adults were waiting for us in front of the school, ready to chase and beat us. I didn't understand why our school was considered segregated if we were the only two African-American kids enrolled. I didn't understand why people would throw bricks at our windows and burn crosses in our front yard. When I would ask my mom, "Why do they hate us?" she'd answer, "I don't know. But you have to love them more than they hate you." Between my two parents, I grew up believing that by investing in relationships, I could change the world.

I went from owning my own candy business at 6-years-old to managing two-thirds of The Coca Cola Company at 37-years-old, and it was in that capacity that I worked to effect change. Despite my success in the corporate world, I was failing as the spiritual leader of my home. I'll never forget when my wife challenged me, asking, "Do you have a personal relationship with Jesus Christ?" Her question upset me. Here I was the youth director of my church - why would she ask me that?

As time went on, I realized that I did not know the Father as I thought I did. For an entire year I prayed, "Father, I want to know who you are." He took me to the book of Genesis and I started all over again. That year, I read from Genesis to Revelation, always with one question in mind: "Father, who are you?" I saw the creator in all of his magnificent glory, a sovereign God who was ruler of all. I saw a promise of Jesus Christ, His enduring faithfulness.

In my second year of study, I read the Bible from Genesis to Revelation again, but with a different question in mind: "Father, who am I?" In return, He revealed to me just how separated I was from His plumb-line. The third year that I read the Bible, I asked, "Jesus, since you are the Savior, who are you?" And after coming to know Jesus, I asked, "What have you designed me for? What is my ultimate purpose?"

I prayed, "Lord, would you use me in a mighty way?" My wife said, "Whoa! Don't pray that prayer. We'll end up in Africa or something." But I wanted to serve Him. I'm a product of discipleship. And so He trained me at Perimeter Church, a church that was built on discipleship. He sent me to Bible Study Fellowship, where I became a discussion leader and then a teaching leader.

I remember sitting in the basement of my

home, undergoing this process of spiritual growth, when God told me to move on from spiritual milk that has been settled; it was time to mature. I asked him, "What does that mean? What is spiritual maturity?" He said, "That you would love Me more than you've ever loved anything because of what I've done on the cross. Every day that you're in doubt, go back to the cross and know that I put My word in your life to change it forever. I put people in your life to change it forever. Invest in people and the world will change forever." I was on the basement floor, saying, "Lord, I've made great progress." And He said to me, "I can't use you at 90%. I need all of you. There's nothing you can do to earn My favor."

All of my life I had lived a performance theology. I thought I could earn God's favor, but He showed me how to fall madly in love with what He's done on the cross. As a result of that love, I am compelled to follow Him no matter the consequence. He has equipped me for works of service and blessed me with a love of business so that I may minister in the world's largest marketplace ministry, Fellowship of Companies for Christ. Business is the largest platform from which to shout: worldwide, there's 90 million businesses, 5 million churches, 2 million educational institutions, and 300,000 missionaries.

What started as a candy business is ending with a prime platform for the Lord. Amen.

Terence Chatmon

Terence brings a diverse, 20-year background in corporate, entrepreneurial and non-profit ministry leadership. Following completion of studies in Marketing at the University of Illinois, Chatmon's corporate business career included leadership positions at Johnson & Johnson, Citibank, and Coca Cola. After authoring a popular Bible-based family enrichment course, Focus on the Family brought him on staff in Colorado Springs as Vice President of Community Impact Outreach. More recently, he served as President of Urban Ministries in Chicago.

Learn More: www.fcci.org

THE COURAGE FOR COMPASSION

Todd Bisio

"Fear not, for I am with you. Be not dismayed,
for I am your God.
I will strengthen you. Yes, I will help you.
I will lift you up with my righteous right hand."
–Isaiah 41:10

Boarding a flight on June 26th, 2006, I thought I had the world all figured out. I had just become the president of a high tech development company. I had a beautiful wife, a young son, extended family, wonderful friends. And we just found out that our second child was on the way. It was on this flight - out of nowhere - that I started feeling weak, numb. I thought, "I've been traveling for four weeks straight. I must be exhausted." When I finally got to Washington, DC, I pressed through the week despite feeling sicker and sicker, weaker and weaker. I was sneezing like crazy during my business meetings. Then I started stumbling around. Still, I met my obligations and flew back home.

That Saturday, while running errands with my wife and son, I kept jerking the car to a stop. My wife asked if everything was okay, and I said,

"You know, it must be fatigue, I'm really not sure." She asked if I wanted her to drive, and I said no. At that point we were only a half-mile away from home. But by the time I entered the garage, I had no feeling in my right foot. We went straight to urgent care, initiating a 10-month long process to determine that I had a chronic disease called multiple sclerosis. MS affects every person differently. Weakness, numbness, fatigue, those were the issues with which I dealt. I figured I was going to overcome MS like I'd overcome everything else in my life up until that point.

Then I had the worst attack I'd ever had. My vision and motor skills weakened. I thought, "How am I going to support my family?" I went into a dark closet and prayed to God. I prayed for His strength and healing. I prayed for a renewed passion for His word, to be filled with the Holy Spirit like never before. And I also prayed that He would give me compassion for others who are dealing MS and other diseases that I had never really thought of before. As I came out of prayer, my vision came back almost instantaneously. My fine motor skills came back within a couple of days. And within a couple of weeks, my fatigue lessened. I've been in remission for seven years now, so praise God for that.

My community, family, and friends gave me additional strength and courage to turn my life over to Christ. I didn't take my prayer lightly: I would serve Him wholeheartedly. He has given me the opportunity to be on the leadership council of the MS Society and to be involved in various ministries as an elder and small group leader at my church. Yet there was one thing that I had forgotten, which was turning my business over to Christ. My co-workers and I worked together on strategic faith-based planning. The goal was to develop our business model as a platform company for Christ; to seek the wisdom that comes from above. It's been tremendous. As we turned control of the business over to the Lord we began to see our company transform. He became the CEO of the company and we became one of the fastest growing companies in our state.

My daughter best summarized what we're trying to do on a daily basis: "Leave the world just a little bit better than it was. Leave the world just a little bit better than you found it. When the sun comes up, I'm only one and you are, too. Soon there'll be others like me and you. We know a word, it's called respect. Give what you expect." God has blessed us in so many ways. We're thankful that He has given us the strength and courage to not only move forward with this disease, but to help and encourage others in our community. Amen.

Todd Bisio

Todd is currently involved in economic development and building strategic relationships focused on helping others connect to opportunities for entrepreneurial success and job creation. Some of his other career highlights include working as the Business Manager for the Office of the Secretary of Defense (OSD) High Energy Laser Joint Technology Office (HEL JTO) as a Schafer Corporation employee, working for Boeing-SVS, Inc. and working on the Air Force Research Laboratories (AFRL) Advanced Electro-Optical Systems (AEOS) Program at the Maui Space Surveillance Site (MSSS). Todd serves on several business and community organizations including, the National Multiple Sclerosis (MS) Society.

THE EVIDENCE ABOUNDS

Thomas Winder

"Seek first the Kingdom of God and His righteousness and all these things shall be added to you."
– Matthew 6:33

I worked myself to the bone achieving the American dream, ensuring that my wife and kids would be fine and dandy on a contractor's salary. I worried and worried, never seeking God first. So when my second wife decided that she didn't want to be a wife *or* a mother, I worked harder, worried more, now with two kids to raise on my own. At the time they were only five and seven. No relatives around. No help whatsoever. I worked and worried and somehow the Lord brought us through. I sold the house, we moved to Albuquerque, and I got a job at Trinity Southwest University.

One Sunday afternoon after church, I chopped down a tree in the backyard. It was the tree from hell, a sequoia with thorns four inches long. I fired up the chain saw and cut that baby up. Only the stump was left. When I bent over to inspect my work, I had a massive heart attack. It felt like one of those movies where the alien bursts out of your chest, horrible pain like you couldn't believe. I was about one hundred feet from the house, so I had to crawl, yelling for help. No one was around. My children were with the neighbors at an arts festival in town. I left a trail of sweat to the house, sometimes crawling, sometimes rolling. My body was waning. I knew that I was dying.

When I finally got to the house, I picked up the phone to call 911. At that exact moment, my ex-wife was on the line. Have you ever made a phone call where it never rings but somebody is on the line? I said, "Get off the phone. I'm trying to get dispatch. I'm having a heart attack." Of course my ex-wife panics. She hangs up, then immediately calls dispatch. I'm trying to call, too, but there she is again. I said, "Get off the phone." By then I can hardly speak. When I get through to a 911 dispatcher, there were no words left. The woman said, "Don't worry. We're on our way. Just don't hang up the phone."

So there I was, in the middle of the living room floor, when I realized that I had a 90-pound Doberman who was going to attack anyone who broke down the door. I crawled to the front door, opened it, and waited on the porch. About then, the ambulance and fire department arrived. They cut my clothes off. They stuck me full of IVs. They put me onto the gurney and into the ambulance.

Right there in the ambulance, I prayed. These guys were doing everything they could for me, but I knew my time was up. So I prayed. I didn't care if these guys could hear me or not. I said, "Lord, if you want to meet me face to face right now, I'm ready. But I have two children who really, really, really, need me." And the Lord answered my prayer. He actually spoke to me in that moment. He said, "Thomas, don't worry. I'm not finished with you." I looked up and saw the EKG machine go flat. My eyes closed and I died. About 20 minutes later, the paramedics pushed a dead man into the hospital. But before any doctor could touch me, I woke up. It shocked the nurses, the doctors. Three days later, I was home and as good as new. Absolutely no repercussions whatsoever, and God gets all the glory. I only missed a week of work. I went back to church the next Sunday. Nobody even knew anything had happened to me.

A month later, Trinity Southwest received a permit to excavate Tall el-Hammam in Jordan, which is the real city of Sedona, of Sodom and Gomorrah. My doctors told me, "You can't go anywhere." I thought, "Are you nuts? I'm going. Oh, I'm going." Soon enough, I was by the Dead Sea working like a mule. For ten years I excavated that site. The evidence that our scriptures are the truth abounds. The Bible is historically accurate. Even the atheist archaeologists have a Bible in their back pockets. It's an enduring reminder that if you seek the Kingdom of God first, if you seek his righteousness first, than all other things come naturally. Amen.

Thomas Winder

Thomas Winder was Professor of Hebraic Studies at Trinity Southwest University & The Museum of Archaeology and Biblical History. Thomas started his Bible education in Jerusalem at the Institute of Holy Land Studies. He has also served as the fundraising director of the "Cities of the Plain Archaeological Project" in Jordan, which is excavating Tall el-Hammam, 'The City of Sodom.'

PROMISES AND PRINCIPLES

Robert Hart

"Be anxious for nothing, but in everything by prayer and supplication, with thanksgiving, let your requests be made known to God; and the peace of God, which surpasses all understanding, will guard your hearts and minds through Christ Jesus."
– Phillippians 4:6-7

What would you give to have peace in your life? To have safety, security, and comfort? I grew up in a family that didn't know the meaning of those words. My mother and father divorced when I was 10-years-old and before I turned 10-and-a-half, my brothers, sisters and I had a stepdad. At first he was Santa dad. He bought us presents and took us places, but later the monster emerged. We experienced his drunken rage up close and personal. I was desperate for peace.

Then I met pastor Greg Wells. Greg showed me, "Hey man, there's a father out there who is absolutely safe, who wants you, who chose you." When he shared the gospel with me, I was like, "Pick me! Pick me, Lord!" And you know, he did pick me. I began to experience some of that peace talked about in Philippians 4:6-7. In following Christ, I could relax, experiencing God's love for the first time in my life.

Of course, I still had periods of anxiety. Around 1994, I had another anxious night. I couldn't sleep at all, so I decided to get up and pray. God kept drawing my heart to Romans 12:2 where Paul encourages us: "Don't be conformed to the image of this world but be transformed by the renewing of your mind." As my heart meditated on that verse, God gave me a vision to be a counselor who used his words in promises and principles. I said, "I'm going to do it, Lord. I'm going to give my life over to you and become a counselor. Teach others how to be free from anxiety, how to transform their lives by renewing their minds."

I spent the next 10 years working hard. About two years in, I became very, very frustrated. I was like, "Lord, why would you give me this vision but prevent me from making it happen?" Enter Greg Wells into my life again. God used this man at strategic points in my life. Greg reminded me of the story of Joseph, how God gave Joseph a vision, but before that vision materialized, he experienced adversity. What Greg said rocked my world: "Robert, do you think Joseph had your attitude when he was a slave? Do you think he had your attitude when he was in prison charged as a sex offender?" It cut me to the core, because the week prior, my own pastor had said to me, "You know, Robert, you seem like you want to be somewhere else. Doesn't God have you right here?"

I began a new journey in my life. "Lord," I said, "if I'm going to be a prisoner, I want to be the best prisoner I can be. I want to be like Joseph. I want to be your trustee right where you've got me." That's when God filled my life with His peace and began to open up doors. I stand before you today in a place of peace because I became the best prisoner for Christ that I could be, not anxious for anything. By prayer and supplication, with thanksgiving, I let my requests be known to God. Thanks to his faithfulness, He guards my heart and mind today. Amen.

Robert Hart

Robert Hart is an LPC Supervisor, serving as the Executive Director at Living Hope Christian Counseling Service since September 2012. He has been licensed as a Professional Counselor since 1999 and has specialized in work related to sexual trauma (both victims and perpetrators) since 2001. He uses faith based counseling skills, as well as trauma informed strategies to help individuals overcome and heal from past trauma.

Learn More: www.livinghopeccs.org

WHY NOT ME?

Martha Speakman

"Now to Him who is able to do exceedingly abundantly above all that we ask or think, according to the power that works in us." – Ephesians 3:20

My life changed forever on March 18th, 1978. It was a beautiful day. Anticipation was in the air. My two-year-old son Tray and I were going to the Citywide Annual Easter Egg Hunt. Josh, my husband, was unable to go that day because he had Army Reserve duty, so it was just the two of us. I was 27-years-old, eight-months pregnant with my second son, and life was great.

It was my turn to run the first egg hunt, so I put Tray in child care. When I went back to pick him up, he wasn't there. I looked everywhere. I started to panic. I ran into a friend of mine who had this frantic look on her face, visibly upset. I said, "What's wrong?" She said, "We found a little boy who drowned in the pond." At that moment my heart dropped. "What was he wearing?" I asked. And she said, "A little blue sailor suit."

That was my son.

I don't remember anything else except sitting in a stupor. I couldn't understand what was going on. This couldn't be happening. Not to me. I was a good Christian girl, blessed to be born into a family of two loving Christian parents. Some of my fondest memories are singing in the church choir with my dad or helping him lead revivals. I was active in the youth group, attended Sunday school and Bible study. I went on to a Christian university where I met my husband. I did everything right. God, where are you?

A month later, our second child Clay was born. I was torn between great joy and great anguish. Every morning, in the fleeting moments before consciousness set in, I didn't feel pain. The rest of the time, I bounced between depression and despair and overwhelming grief. I would periodically run into Clay's room because I was so afraid that something would happen to him. God saw my pain and sent someone unexpected into my life. My best friend called me and said, "I want you to talk to my mom." I said, "Your mom's a nice lady, but I don't know why you want me to talk to her." She said, "You have a lot in common. She lost a son 30 years ago." I was stunned. I knew Edith Kirkpatrick. She was a wonderful Christian woman with joy in her life. It made no sense to me. I could never imagine feeling joy again.

Over time, Edith showed me who the God of the Bible is, the God who walks through suffering with us, who doesn't protect us from it. I don't know where I was when I read all those Bible stories, but somehow the suffering part had never registered with me. As God began to minister to me through Edith, I grew to know the Lord in a whole new way. He did not abandon me. He was walking through suffering with me. I would cry my eyes out over this anguish, cry out to God, "Why?" But as Edith said, "You have to go from why me, to why *not* me?"

Five months after Tray died, I got a phone call from my mom in tears. My dad had just been diagnosed with terminal cancer and had six months to live. My dad who was my hero, who wasn't even 60 years old, was dying and I couldn't do a thing about it. We prayed. I knew God had the power to heal but it wasn't to be. My dad went home to be with the Lord 11 months after we lost our son.

The next few months turned into years. By then my husband Josh and I had three children – a son and two beautiful daughters. Everyone thought we were the perfect couple because we were strong. We'd beaten the odds, we weren't going to divorce like 95% of people who lose children. But we were only getting by. At heart, we had grieved separately. I cried, my husband worked at cheering me up. He would come home whistling a song, but instead of cheering me it made me angry. I wanted him to cry with me. He wanted me to quit moping. The crack in our marriage grew bigger and bigger despite the fact that we were both youth leaders in our church.

Eight years after we lost our son, my husband told me he didn't think he wanted to be married anymore. I knew our marriage wasn't great, but this was a blow that I couldn't take. "What if we go to counseling?" I asked. "We can get help, work on our marriage." His silence was deafening. Finally he said, "I don't know." At that point I left the room. "God, this is it," I prayed. "I can't take anymore. I can't fix this." I cried out to Him not in anger but in total desperation. I said, "Lord, you are my only hope. I'm not at the end of my rope. I'm free falling." As He spoke to me He said, "Find your hope in Me." I realized that as much as I loved my son, my dad, my husband, my marriage, they were not my hope. They could never be my hope. God was my only hope.

My husband and I were separated for several weeks before we decided to work on our marriage. God opened my eyes to see Josh as God saw him. Not someone who wanted to tear up our marriage or hurt me or abandon his family, but someone who was hurting as deeply as I was hurting. Someone who needed healing as deeply as I needed healing. There'd be times when he would lay his head in my lap and say some very hard things that I needed to hear. In my flesh I wanted to lash out or call a divorce attorney, but

God allowed me to see Josh as He did. He buffered my heart so that I could hear what I needed to hear. He also showed me that I was responsible for my part in the breakdown of our marriage, and that I needed to ask for forgiveness.

Over the next two years, God brought us together in a way that I never could have imagined. He took us out of the ashes and transformed us. He restored our family. "To Him who is able to do exceedingly, abundantly above all that we could ever ask or think through the power that works within us." To Him be the glory forever and ever. Amen.

Martha Speakman

Martha Speakman joined the New Mexico Baptist Foundation in April 2000 as director of the Church Finance Corporation (CFC), the church lending division of the foundation. She currently serves as Senior Vice President overseeing CFC operations, providing financing, budgeting and consulting services to churches in nine western states.

Contact: williamjspeakman@gmail.com

OPEN DOOR

Linda Pena

"But as for you, you meant evil against me;
but God meant it for good, in order to
bring it about as it is this day,
to save many people alive."
– Genesis 50:20

As a child, I saw what drug addiction does to families, the chaos and the drama. I saw my uncles fight, my aunts cry, my grandmother cry, my mom cry. There's nothing worse than a mother's cry, a mother's broken heart. I'll never forget it. At 12-years-old my father died of a drug overdose, then my uncle committed suicide. I came to hate drug addicts and drug dealers. When I saw homeless people on the side of the road, I had no empathy for them. "They ask for that life," I thought.

Then God humbled me. I was a court clerk working on a high-profile murder trial in Las Vegas, Nevada. Two teenagers who were under the influence of methamphetamine killed their friend. I shared the story with my daughters as a warning. Deep down I thought, "I work in a courtroom. There's no way my daughters would use drugs." But methamphetamine doesn't care what you do for a living. It has no socio-economic boundaries.

My daughter was introduced to methamphetamine in her junior high school hallway. All of her friends were doing it and she wanted to, too. I saw the pattern: staying up late, bringing home freaks and creeps. My daughter was turning pretty freaky, too. Her teacher called to tell me the school found pot in her backpack. Or she smelled like alcohol. Or she ditched class. I knew something was seriously wrong, but I didn't want to face it. I was still working this trial, stressed out from the stories of broken-hearted mothers, their awful sobbing cries. I was in denial that I was one of those mothers, too.

Prepared to finally confront my daughter, I went straight to her room after work one day. But she was gone. Her TV was gone. Her VCR and stereo were gone. I knew immediately that she had run away. In those days we didn't have cell phones, so I found her little address book and called all of her friends. Not one of them would tell me where she was. Day one came and went. So did day two. Day three. The guilt was devastating; the last time I saw my daughter, we fought. I didn't get to say I love you. I just wanted to hold her. All the while, I'm working this trial. The gruesome photos were overwhelming. "My baby's out there on the streets of Sin City," I thought. She was only 14-years-old.

Finally, on day eight, I'm so overwhelmed I can't function. I got on my knees and said, "God, bring my baby home. Be the middle man. Just tell her to come home. I know that she's hurting. I know that she's lost and scared." I prayed and prayed until I fell asleep. When I woke up, I prayed again. "God, I can't do this. Please tell her, wherever she is, that the door to the church is always open." I slept well for the first time in eight days.

I woke up to a phone call at 6 o'clock in the morning. A woman said, "Is this Linda, Darlene's mother?" I was so scared to answer, afraid that this was the dreaded call. But I said, "Yes, this is Linda." And she said, "I have your daughter. She's okay, but she's going to need medical attention." We made arrangements to meet 30 miles away at a parking lot. When I pulled up, I almost didn't recognize my daughter. Her beautiful long black hair had been shaved off. She couldn't walk. She couldn't talk. She was drooling. I asked, "Where did you find her?" The woman said, "It's the strangest thing. I found her in the church. I clean the church. I just don't know how she got in there."

At the hospital, the doctors hooked my daughter up to an IV and kept her overnight for observation. I prayed and prayed and prayed. The following morning, they said, "One more day, if she would've been gone just more day, she would've died from dehydration." She didn't eat, she didn't drink, she didn't sleep for nine consecutive days.

I took her home and held my traumatized daughter in my arms. She slept and slept for seven days. Finally, on the seventh day, she was able to speak. "How did you end up in the church?" I asked. She said, "Mom, I don't know what happened. My friends dropped me off at a convenience store and I got lost. I was scared. And then I heard your voice. You told me to go to a church, that there's always a door open for me." She said she saw a cross lit up on the hill. She followed it to the church. The back door was open, so she laid down on a pew. The woman found her the following morning.

I thought that my daughter had learned her lesson, but methamphetamine has a strong hold; soon enough she was back on the rollercoaster. We battled it out for the next 10 years. During that time, I worked as my own DEA. I parked in alleyways and watched. Every time a dealer came to the house, I chased them away. But I got so tired. It took its toll on me.

My daughter brought two beautiful babies into the world, and I had to take them away from her.

One day, my daughter came over to visit her children. She hadn't slept for days. She collapsed on the floor, fell asleep in front of the doorway so that you had to climb over her to get outside. Her 2-year-old daughter held her hand and said, "Mommy, wake up. Please wake up."

I cried and cried. I cried like my grandmother cried and all of those moms in the courtroom cried. I said, "God, take her. Take her and end this once and for all because we can't do it anymore." And I promised God that whatever His decision, I would reach out and help families who are suffering from methamphetamine. I would see drug addicts and homeless people through God's eyes. "Give me strength," I prayed. The following morning, my daughter was still asleep. She slept in front of that door for 18 hours. I said, "God, you take her." I chased her out of the house, stepped back, and let God do his work.

Finally, my daughter couldn't take it either. She wanted to commit suicide. She got on her knees and said, "God, I just can't do this anymore." And then the phone rang. She didn't follow through. The next time she attempted suicide, someone knocked on her door. After exhausting every option grace overcame. Darlene surrendered and let God into her heart. It's been nine years since my daughter gave her life to God. "But as for you, you meant evil against me; but

God meant it for good, in order to bring it about as it is this day, to save many people's lives." Amen.

Linda Pena

After a ten-year struggle for her daughter to get clean and stay clean, Linda Peña contacted a local television talk show and offered to appear on the show to discuss the horrors of methamphetamine. Her appearance resulted in a documentary, produced by a company called Global Studio and financed by a nonprofit community-based organization called Secret Witness. Peña became an advocate for parents who were suffering from their child's addiction by starting a chapter of the national organization of Mothers Against Meth-Amphetamine (MAMA).

Contact: lakegirl702@gmail.com

GOD OF SPORT

Scott Warman

"One thing I know: that though I was blind, now I see."
– John 9:25

Growing up, I didn't particularly like school. It was something that I tolerated. But sports? It was all that I wanted to do. Something took over. I really fell in love. I played many, many sports throughout my early years, and as time went on, I became convinced that I would become a professional football player.

I had my first setback in high school, an injury that really changed my life. I hurt my leg, an anterior cruciate medial-collateral tear, which led me to begin weight training. I could strengthen my body and build that leg back up. With my dream back on track, I accepted an opportunity to play football at Marshall University in Huntington, West Virginia. Yet I struggled to play at that level. I shifted my focus to competitive lifting, and as a senior in college I competed in the collegiate nationals. It was at that competition that I found my true niche as an athlete. Before I knew it, I was an alternate on the USA team. Everything revolved around lifting. People would ask me, "Scott, how can you be so passionate about this?" All I could say was, "A bird flies, a fish swims, and Scott Warman lifts."

As I look back now, I see how egotistical and narrow-minded I was, but at the time it was perfectly natural. Lifting fulfilled everything that life had to offer. I wanted power and adulation and respect. I couldn't get enough of the international limelight. Lifting became my god, and I fed that god constantly. For many, many years I would get up twice in the middle of the night to eat protein shakes. I would do just about anything to maintain my weight at 300 pounds. It was a chore to eat 14,000 calories a day, but I more than welcomed that chore. It was as good as life could get. I was lifing full-time and coaching college athletes. And yet I knew that my identity, my satisfaction in life, revolved around my performance. I remember thinking how sad it's going to be when one day I'm no longer able to compete. "What will I do with all of that time?" I thought.

After my second divorce, I came to my lowest of lows. Getting up in the morning, showering, and eating exhausted me. I just wanted to close my eyes and have it be over. And so our divine Heavenly King reached out to me. As I struggled through that divorce, I thought of my parents who'd taught me not to quit, to keep pushing.

With them in mind, I persevered. I reached out to God in a way that I never did before. I asked for his help, and God answered that prayer with an insatiable desire to read His word. The scales began to fall from my eyes as I experienced God's holiness, the grace and mercy that he has on us, and the substitution that he took for my sinful life. I was overwhelmed with love for Jesus Christ.

I didn't know it, but there was another storm brewing that would really test me. A virus attacked my heart. I had atrial fibrillation, which accelerated my heart rate. I was put on life support; my heart had to be reprogrammed twice. That was a difficult, difficult time.

Looking back, I believe it was God's way of taking my idolatry away from me. He took my strength and my muscle and left just me. It was a hard road, but I praise Him for that, because thereafter I clung to the cross, depending completely on God. And doors began to open. I got involved with the ministry. I became a chaplain with Gideons. I began to do Evangelism, teaching and preaching. Best of all, I no longer feared the future. I don't necessarily know what it will bring, but I see the hand of God upon me. I have purpose. "Though I was blind, now I see." Amen.

Scott Warman

Over a 12-year span from 1987 to 1999, Warman was an eight-time heavyweight world-champion powerlifter, as well as a 10-time heavyweight national-champion. His all-time best competition lifts included: squat (leg strength), 964 pounds; deadlift (back strength), 860 pounds; and bench press (upper body strength), 529 pounds. In 1999, Powerlifting USA magazine named Warman the best lifter of the 1990s. A former UTEP strength coach, 1989 1994, with a master's degree in exercise science, he currently owns and operates Warman's New Pro Gym.

ERICH THE CHRISTIAN SLAYER

Erich Soiles

Then the Lord said,
"I am Jesus who you are persecuting.
It is hard for you to kick against the goads."
–Acts 9:5

I was the kid in Sunday school who got in trouble for asking why the lions didn't eat the zebras on the ark. We were diehard Greek Orthodox: baptised in a golden bowl, church every Sunday. I learned to kneel, sit, stand, kneel, sit, stand. I didn't learn much else, unfortunately. Mostly just fear. My childhood was rough.

My mother was an alcoholic, a binge drinker, the worst kind because I never knew what to expect. She attempted suicide several times, twice in front of me, but didn't succeed. My father was the Tasmanian Devil. He beat my mother and me on a daily basis both physically and mentally. In bed at night I'd pray, "Please God, take this man away from me. Kill him. I can't take it anymore." But that never happened. That's when I started to hate God.

As a young adult, I had a lot of pain and suffering, so I turned to drugs and alcohol. A *lot* of drugs and alcohol. Snorted it, smoked it, drank it, ate it, anything that I could get my hands on to numb my pain was fair game. Drugs elevated my Christian hatred to another level. If I could smell a Christian at a party, I would go after him. I would attack him.

My wife, too, had a very rough childhood. I fell in love with her on first sight. I loved her tremendously, but she had issues that she was dealing with. She was using drugs and alcohol well into our marriage. It came to a point where I told her, "You need to stop or the kids and I are going to leave." She didn't stop.

One day, she came to me and said, "I'm going to become a Christian. I'm going to go to church. I'm going to change my life." I was like, "What? I'm Erich, the Christian Slayer. How can that be?" And she says, "I had an inspiration." I was like, "You had a conversation with God? God came down from the sky and sat next to you and talked to you?" She said, "No, Erich. I was inspired. I had a feeling, a gift."

And then it happened. I watched her transform into this beautiful, tremendous Christian woman who was loving and patient, who led by example, who never shoved her beliefs down my throat. It was incredible. She had something that I wanted, but of course I wasn't going to tell her that. See, I went to church with my wife, telling her that I was just there to support her, but I was curious. What was this Christian life all about? I wanted to see it for myself.

One day before church started, I was sitting on the couch talking to my wife when I made eye contact with pastor Kent Tucker. I'll never forget it. I could tell that he was trouble with a capital T. He got about five feet from me before I told him, "Stop right there. No, no, no. I'm only here to support my wife. I don't believe in any of this God stuff." And he said, "Hey, that's a great reason for us to go to lunch!" I thought, he doesn't know I'm the Christian Slayer. I'm going to take him down.

When I got home, I Googled everything I could on why God wasn't real in preparation for my lunch with Kent. But he answered my questions with scripture, patience. Every time I was like, "Alright, Kent are you ready," he would say, "Here, read this." A year of going to lunch with Kent every Thursday transformed my life. We sat down one Thursday like we always did and I told him, "Kent, I want to be baptised. I'm ready." We went out to my truck and said a prayer together. I gave my life to Christ at that very moment. It was like 10,000 pounds had been lifted off of my shoulders. I cried for what seemed like hours.

Shortly after I got baptised, it was incredible: I saw God at 60 miles an hour. But I have to set up the story: I am an incredible creature of habit. I do the same thing, the same way, every day. Brush my teeth the same way, store my keys the same way, put on my clothes the same way. It keeps me sane. One morning I was taking my daughter to school like I did every morning, always early, never late. Only this day we were running late. That stressed me out. We approached a four-way stop when a Suburban driving 60 miles an hour ran the stop sign. If I would have been on time, we would've been killed.

I'd talked to God a lot before I decided to become a Christian. I told Him, "If you hurt me, if you hurt my family, you'll never win me over, ever." I knew as I pulled into the school parking lot that God was opening my eyes. What if my mother succeeded in commiting suicide? What would I have become? What if my father died as I prayed for him to die? How would a 10-year-old child live with that? What if my wife never had her inspiration? And what about Kent? How did I just happen to make eye contact with Kent that day? Was it a coincidence? I think not. My life is still challenging, but by the grace of God, I am the happiest I've ever been. Amen.

Erich Soiles

Erich was born in Phoenix, AZ, and had a very difficult home life. At the age of eighteen, he left home and went directly into the workforce. He excelled in leadership and sales and started several small businesses. His latest venture in commercial construction has been successful for the last 10 years, and continues today. He met my wife Kelly in 1998 and married her in 2004. They live in Rancho Cucamonga and have 3 wonderful children together.

THE DARE

Charlene Haddad Brown

"And they overcame him by the blood of the Lamb and by the word of their testimony, and they did not love their lives to the death."
– Revelation 12:11

My dad is Middle Eastern, from Amman, Jordan. My mom is Italian-American. That's a pretty uncommon mix, I know. Growing up, my dad held strongly to his Arab customs, which for his three children translated into straight A's, remaining pure until marriage, and arranged marriage after high school. As the only daughter, I felt tremendous pressure. My dad was abusive both physically and emotionally to my mom and myself; my brothers had it easier.

The abuse got so bad that after 11 years of marriage, my mom fled. We stayed in numerous women's shelters, eventually ending up in California. A year into our new life, my mom got really sick. She had a nerve disorder that required brain surgery. With no one to care for her three kids, she had to send us back to our dad. During my mom's surgery and recovery, my dad took us to court and forced us to tell the judge that we wanted to live with him. I knew that my life was going to be a nightmare. My dad worked 12-hour shifts six days a week, and so I was left to assume the mother role. At 10-years-old, I cleaned the house, prepared the meals, and tucked my brothers in at night. No mall, no makeup, no friends. I had to grow up fast.

Because my dad was away so often, he used intimidation tactics to control me. If he found out that I was talking to a boy, he threatened to kill me. In the Middle East, honor killings are customary. If a woman brings shame onto her family, the means of restoring honor is to kill the woman. I grew hostile toward my dad. At 13-years-old, I rebelled by having sex. I came home with hickeys on my neck, freaking out. How could I possibly hide them? That moment was the only time in my life that I've ever contemplated suicide, but I couldn't bring myself to do it. When my dad got home, he woke me up and interrogated me about my day. I told him I was with girlfriends, but he saw the hickeys and went ballistic.

He cornered me in the bathroom, a loaded gun pointed to my head. I told him, "Pull the trigger," because I didn't want to suffer the consequences if I lived. My eight-year-old brother was in the background screaming, sobbing, "Dad, dad, don't do it." My brother saved my life that night, though I received a brutal beating. After that, my dad harassed me every day. "Who did this to you?" he asked over and over again. "I'm going to kill him."

It got so unbearable that I ran away. I was alone, 13-years-old, in New York City. After a few days, I finally got a hold of my mom. I said, "Mom, I'm coming to live with you."

A New Yorker in California, I thought I was hard core. My friends used to joke, "You're a double threat, Arab and Italian. That's like Mafia terrorist." I was a caged animal finally let out into the wild. I smoked weed, drank, and became promiscuous. At 14-years-old, as a sophomore in high school, I discovered that I was pregnant. I thought, "This wasn't supposed to happen to me. I'm scheduled to graduate my junior year, then go on to an Ivy League college and med school." A kid would change everything. My mom would be disappointed. My dad would kill me for sure.

I made an appointment at the abortion clinic. In California, the age of consent is 12-years-old. I didn't have to pay a fee because I was a minor without my parents' consent. They gave me a pill to help me relax, but it never kicked in. I was in a cold white room on a hard metal table, people in white coats murmuring around me, but all I heard were my own thoughts: "Am I really going to go through with this? What else can I do?" Then I heard a vacuum sound. I felt awful pain in my stomach. I whispered, "I'm a murderer," but the nurse reassured me that I was doing the right thing. I knew it was a lie because I left more empty and broken than when I arrived.

The clinic sent me home with a packet of papers that I shoved under my mattress. That's where I left my feelings about the abortion: under the mattress. I went on to meet my high school sweetheart and graduate at 16-years-old with a 4.0 GPA. The plan was Ivy Leagues and med school, only that never happened. I didn't have the same ambition as before. Later, I would learn that a lack of drive is common among post-abortive girls. At the time, I simply settled for community college. A few years later, my high school sweetheart and I celebrated a pregnancy. We married. Everything was going so well.

One night, I was home alone watching the church channel. The story drew me in. I thought, "That's my life, right there." By the end of the segment I was weeping. I was like, "Whoa, what's wrong with me?" The host of the show gave an invitation to follow Jesus and I said, "You know what? I've tried everything else. I tried to find love in my dad and drugs and sex and partying with no results. Why not try Jesus?" And so I did. I gave my life to Him that night. My husband, son, and I were baptized shortly thereafter. God just rocked my world.

Years pass. My brother's girlfriend calls to tell me that she's pregnant. She says, "Your brother doesn't want it. He wants to 'take care of it' tomorrow." For the first time in 14 years, I share my experience with her. "It's not worth it," I tell her. "Every day for the rest of your life you're going to wonder if it was a boy or a girl. You're going to wonder what your baby would've looked like. Every year that passes, you're going to think, 'My baby would've been this old, this old, this old.' And when you *do* have children? When you see how beautiful and amazing they are, you can't fathom an abortion."

I invited her to church and she came. We had a guest speaker but I didn't know who he was. It was Minister Ray Comfort, and he presented a documentary about abortion. I thought, "God, did you plan this out?" My brother's girlfriend cried and in that moment I realized that the enemy of my soul tried to fill me with shame and guilt, but God turned it around for good. He saved a life that night. In November of 2012, my amazing nephew Christian was born.

If the world has beat you up, if you're just hanging on by a thread, you have a heavenly Father who loves you so much. He knows every pain that you go through. I lost my child and He knew exactly how I felt because He lost His, too. He sent His son to die on the cross for my sin and for yours. So I will leave you with a dare. If you've tried everything - drugs, partying, sex, whatever promises fulfillment but doesn't deliver - I dare you to try Jesus Christ. I guarantee He won't disappoint you. Amen.

Charlene Hadad Brown

Charlene is a mother of two beautiful children and married her high school sweetheart. She is passionately pro-life and is dedicated to sharing her abortion testimony to further the kingdom. Her hope is to shine the light of Jesus as she currently works for a crisis pregnancy center.

Contact: chaddadbrown@yahoo.com

Testify World

Testify World is a Global Community of Kingdom Builders Sharing the Transformational Power of Jesus Christ.

Our Mission: "Making the Invisible Kingdom VISIBLE"

Connect with Testify World…

Website:	TestifyWorld.com
Facbook:	facebook.com/TestifyWorld
Twitter:	twitter.com/TestifyWorld
Google +:	+TestifyWorld1
YouTube:	youtube.com/TestifyWorld
Email:	unashamed@testifyworld.com

Together We Are Making
The Invisible Kingdom VISIBLE!

WHAT NOW??

Dear Readers,

If after reading any of these incredible true stories of the transformational power of Jesus Christ you find that you have not yet begun a personal relationship with your Creator, here are a few things to help you take the next step to begin your exciting adventure. 1) Pray, 2) Read the Bible daily and grow in your faith, 3) Get connected to other Christians, 4) Share your story.

PRAY

Prayer is simply talking to God. It doesn't have to be formal or fancy. Just talk to him about everything going on in your life (He already knows anyway, so talk to him about it). Begin your relationship by praying to ask God to come into your life and forgive you for your failures. Here are a few suggested prayers.

A Simple Prayer:

Dear God, I want to know You personally. I confess that I am a sinner, because I am far from perfect, and I need Your forgiveness. Thank You for sending your Son, Jesus Christ, to die on the cross for my sins. I open up my heart to receive Jesus as my personal Lord and Savior. Thank You for giving me a new hope and a new life, just by believing in You. And thank You for giving me eternal life. Please take control of my life and make me the kind of person whom you created me to be. Amen.

A Special Prayer for Jewish People:

(The Bible says Christ came first for the Jew, and then the Gentile--everyone who is NOT Jewish. Many people don't realize Jesus was Jewish. So here's a sample prayer if you are Jewish and want to begin an eternal relationship with your Messiah.)

Dear God of Abraham, Isaac and Jacob, I confess that I have sinned and separated myself from You. I thank you for providing the blood of atonement for me in Messiah/Yeshua. I choose now to put my trust in You, Yeshua, as my Savior, so that I can know you and embrace Your Shalom now and forever. Please take control of my life so that I can live the life of purpose which you created me to live. Amen.

Read the Bible for Yourself

The Bible is your roadmap to life. A rich, living manuscript. Study it and make it a part of your daily life. After you've asked God to come into your life, pick up a Bible and get to know all about Him and the plans he has for you. A great place to start is in the NEW TESTAMENT reading Matthew, Mark, Luke and John. Where to go next?

See below as we've included an excerpt from the book *How to Talk About Jesus without Freaking Out* on "How Not to be Overwhelmed Reading the Bible."

Get Connected to other Believers

Find a local church who teaches from the Bible. Visit a few in your area and see what they offer you for connecting with others and building relationships with like-minded Christians. There are so many churches from large mega-churches to small home churches. We just encourage you to find a group of believers who encourage you to keep reading the Bible yourself as well.

Share Your Story

Just like the people who shared their true story here in *An Unashamed Life*, we encourage you to begin telling others your story of how God reached out and revealed himself to you. Pick up a copy of the book *How to Talk About Jesus without Freaking Out* and let us teach you how to tell YOUR story effectively to anyone, anytime in just three minutes, one minute, or even in a 140 character tweet. It's invigorating to be able to communicate to others what God has done for you!

If you've taken this step in your life we'd love to hear from you!

Email Us: unashamed@testifyworld.com

Here's to your new life in Christ!

How Not to Be Overwhelmed Reading the Bible

- **First and Always:** Ask God for understanding and insight. (Some call this *prayer.*) It was His idea to write the Bible in the first place, so we might as well ask Him to help us to understand it!
- **What to Know:** The Bible is a collection of sixty-six books written by numerous people who have had firsthand encounters with the living, personal God. It is split into two parts: the Old Testament and the New Testament. The Old Testament includes the account of Creation, the history of Israel, and many prophecies of the coming Messiah. The New Testament gives God's plan for man and the fulfillment of every Messianic prophecy in the person of Jesus Christ.
- **Where to begin:** The best place to begin reading is in the Gospels – the first four books of the New Testament. Matthew, Mark, Luke, and John give firsthand accounts of the life of Jesus. We recommend that a new reader begin with the Gospel of John, the clearest overview of the Bible. Then go back to Matthew and read the entire *New* Testament, followed by the *Old* Testament.

Reading for Bible History

- ***GENESIS:*** If you're a person who must start at the beginning, Genesis tells how God showed Himself in the creation of the world and the birth of the nation Israel. In Genesis 3:15, God foreshadows the future revelation of Himself in His son, the Messiah. Its fulfillment is best described in the book of John.
- ***GOSPEL OF JOHN:*** This is a great summary of the life of Jesus. It's only about twenty-five pages long. The

entire Gospel is best summed up in chapter three.

- ***EXODUS:*** Moses leads the people out of Egypt to Mount Sinai where God gives him the Ten Commandments. In the book of Exodus, the celebration of the Passover foreshadows Jesus.
- ***ACTS:*** Keeping in mind the Israelites' struggle to return to the Promised Land, read how the faith of these same people was established with the coming of Jesus as their Messiah.

Reading the Bible for Theology

- ***ROMANS:*** Paul answers the "big" questions of Christian life, including the issues of hope, strength, sin, perseverance, and grace.
- ***PHILIPPIANS:*** A letter written to new Christians on how to lead a life that is pleasing to God.
- ***EPHESIANS:*** Another terrific instruction letter on Christian conduct.
- ***HEBREWS:*** See how throughout the history of the nation of Israel God has always rewarded those who persevere in their life and in their belief in Him.
- ***REVELATION:*** Read only chapters 1 and 22 if you are a new Christian. In these two chapters Jesus talks about His return. The rest of Revelation is pretty much heavy-duty prophecy told in allegories and images.

Reading for Wisdom and Help

- ***A PROVERB A DAY KEEPS THE FOOL AWAY:*** One of the best success manuals ever in print is in the Old Testament. Proverbs – the book of wisdom – has thirty-one chapters. In addition to your daily devotions, it's a wonderful idea to read the chapter that corresponds to the day of the month in which you are reading.

- ***PSALMS – THE PRAYER BOOK OF ANCIENT CHRISTIANS:*** The Psalms have been used as a prayer and songbook for Christians since the days of its author, King David. If you want to learn how to pray, Psalms is a great place to go.

There is Something for Everyone

Here is where to find some of the best biographies:

* Adam and Eve (Genesis1-6)
* Noah (Genesis 6-9)
* Abraham (Genesis 11-25)
* Jacob (genesis 25-29)
* Joseph (Genesis 37-50)
* Moses (Exodus-Deuteronomy)
* Ruth (the book of Ruth)
* David (1Samuel 16; 1 Kings 2:10; Psalms)
* Solomon (1 Kings 1-11, Proverbs)
* Esther (the book of Esther)
* Job (the book of Job)
* And most importantly: Jesus (Matthew-John)

CPSIA information can be obtained
at www.ICGtesting.com
Printed in the USA
FSOW01n0032250915
11486FS

9 780984 922055